US Air Force/TSgt Miguel Lara III

Strategic Bombers

Nuclear Deterrence to Close Air Support

Today's strategic bombers are operated by just three primary air arms: the Peoples Liberation Army Air Force of China, Russia's Air and Space Force Long-Range Aviation service (Dal'naya Aviatsia), and the US Air Force.

In general, strategic bomber aircraft are unlike all other aircraft in the respective nation's inventories.

Each type is designed to carry multiple weapons, including nuclear weapons, to wreak havoc on the assigned targets of an enemy state. During the wars in Afghanistan and Iraq, US Air Force B-1B Lancer and B-52H Stratofortress bombers were also tasked with providing close air support to coalition troops providing long periods of loiter time with plenty of precision-guided weapons available.

Strategic bombers range from the eight-engine B-52 Stratofortress and turboprop powered Tu-95 Bear, B-2 and B-21 stealthy beasts to the supersonic B-1B and Tu-160 Blackjack.

As well as coverage of the aircraft types that fall under the title 'strategic bombers' we've taken a look at the units that fly and support the US Air Force B-1B, B-2 and B-52H with overviews of operations and training. There's also an extensive section on the Russian Tu-22 *Backfire*, Tu-95 *Bear* and Tu-160 *Blackjack* aircraft in service with the Dal'naya Aviatsia, and their use in Putin's abhorrent war against Ukraine.

Most types of bomber aircraft are nasty looking machines with even nastier consequences when sent into combat, they are, as designed, harbingers of destruction.

Strategic Bombers: Nuclear Deterrence to Close Air Support provides details and insight of all the heavy bombers in service today.

Mark Ayton

CONTENTS

US Air Force/Airman 1st Class Christina Bennett

US Air Force/Airman 1st Class Jesse Jenny

Alexander Mladenov

Chinese internet

ISBN: 978 1 80282 765 1
Editor: Mark Ayton
Senior editor, specials: Roger Mortimer
Email: roger.mortimer@keypublishing.com
Cover design: Steve Donovan
Design: SJmagic DESIGN SERVICES, India
Advertising Sales Manager: Brodie Baxter
Email: brodie.baxter@keypublishing.com
Tel: 01780 755131
Advertising Production: Debi McGowan
Email: debi.mcgowan@keypublishing.com

SUBSCRIPTION/MAIL ORDER
Key Publishing Ltd, PO Box 300, Stamford,
Lincs, PE9 1NA
Tel: 01780 480404
Subscriptions email:
subs@keypublishing.com
Mail Order email: orders@keypublishing.com
Website: www.keypublishing.com/shop

PUBLISHING
Group CEO: Adrian Cox
Publisher, Books and Bookazines:
Jonathan Jackson
Published by
Key Publishing Ltd, PO Box 100, Stamford,
Lincs, PE9 1XQ
Tel: 01780 755131
Website: www.keypublishing.com

PRINTING
Precision Colour Printing Ltd, Haldane,
Halesfield 1, Telford, Shropshire. TF7 4QQ

DISTRIBUTION
Seymour Distribution Ltd, 2 Poultry Avenue,
London, EC1A 9PU
Enquiries Line: 02074 294000.

The Mighty Eighth

Mark Ayton details what a strategic bomber is and profiles the largest operator,
Air Force Global Strike Command's Eighth Air Force.

> "Aside from the US, only China and Russia also operate strategic bombers. Both nations don't discuss their strategic bomber forces too often."

EIGHTH AIR FORCE WINGS

Active-Duty		
2nd Bomb Wing and 307th Bomb Wing (Reserve)	Barksdale Air Force Base, Louisiana	B-52H
5th Bomb Wing	Minot Air Force Base, North Dakota	B-52H
7th Bomb Wing	Dyess Air Force Base, Texas	B-1B
28th Bomb Wing	Ellsworth Air Force Base, South Dakota	B-1B
509th Bomb Wing and 131st Bomb Wing (Air National Guard)	Whiteman Air Force Base, Missouri	B-2

The term strategic bomber refers to a medium- to long-range aircraft designed to destroy strategic targets such as infrastructure, military installations, and factories. American B-1B and B-52H strategic bombers were and can be used for tactical missions, such as providing close air support to friendly forces during the war in Afghanistan. Aside from the US, only China and Russia also operate strategic bombers. Both nations don't discuss their strategic bomber forces too often. Consequently, the focus of this introduction is devoted to the biggest operator of strategic bombers, America's Air Force Global Strike Command or AFGSC.

AFGSC is a major command with responsibility for two legs of America's nuclear triad: intercontinental ballistic missiles and 66 nuclear-capable bombers. AFGSC is also responsible for nuclear command, control, and communications capabilities while simultaneously accomplishing the conventional global strike mission.

Since September 29, 2017, Air Forces Strategic – Air (AFSTRAT-Air) serves as the full-time air component to US Strategic Command (USSTRATCOM) with responsibility for its air missions.

The Joint-Global Strike Operations Center (J-GSOC) co-located at Barksdale serves as the central command and control node for all operations within AFGSC, orchestrating warfighting, and readiness activities for the Commander, AFSTRAT-Air.

J-GSOC comprises the Joint Air Operations Center (JAOC) which handles the conventional portion of the command's mission, and the Joint Nuclear Operations Center which handles the nuclear portion of the AFGSC's mission.

The JAOC, designated the 608th Air Operations Center, plans, directs, commands, controls, monitors, and assesses long-range strike missions. It has responsibility for executing USSTRATCOM's air tasking cycle through all phases of conflict in support of the J-GSOC, Bomb Wings and Air Force Global Strike Command.

Eighth Air Force is one of two active-duty numbered air forces in AFGSC with more than 20,000 active-duty, Air National Guard and Reserve airmen assigned.

The Eighth Air Force has three active-duty wings, two Total Force Integration wings and one detachment assigned (see table). It controls long-range B-1B Lancer, B-2 Spirit and B-52 Stratofortress bombers from bases throughout the United States.

BOMBER TASK FORCES

AFGSC's conventional tasking includes Bomber Task Force (BTF) missions. These are usually flown from either home stations in the United States or from forward locations, primarily RAF Fairford, England in the European theatre and Andersen Air Force Base, Guam in the Indo-Pacific theatre.

BTF missions enable airmen to conduct operations throughout the world at short notice to help maintain global stability and security while enabling the units involved to gain familiarity of flying missions in different regions.

Long-planned, BTF missions are not conducted in response to any current political event in either Europe or the Indo-Pacific theatres but accomplish tactical and strategic objectives.

Strategically, they demonstrate to the world the US Air Force's ability to operate with agility. Tactically, they increase bomber force lethality, readiness, and experience across the force.

In accordance with the National Defense Strategy's objectives of strategic predictability and operational unpredictability, the US Air Force has modified its force employment model to enable strategic bombers to operate from a broad array of worldwide locations with greater operational resilience.

During BTF deployments to either Fairford or Andersen, airmen get opportunities to work with their counterparts from allied and partner nations, and to focus on the full spectrum of military operations. This in turn provides opportunities to develop the integral elements of agile combat employment (ACE), either working with new entities to provide the strategic strike capabilities or change how the air force conducts missions to become more agile.

ACE is a proactive and reactive operational scheme of manoeuvre executed within threat timelines to increase survivability while generating combat power. Bomber operations will utilise the ACE concept, dependent on combatant command requirements.

Other BTF missions have demonstrated the ability to operate in the Arctic region, an important capability for supporting US European Command initiatives, and fulfil objectives in the 2018 National Defense Strategy which reoriented the US military's focus from the Middle East to near-peer challenges in Asia and Europe. This has included short notice operations flown from Eielson Air Force Base, Alaska to anywhere within the EUCOM area of responsibility.

PLANNING AND EXECUTION

Each BTF mission is requested by a combatant command through USSTRATCOM to meet that command's individual need.

The J-GSOC, is the operational arm of Air Force Global Strike Command, which is a crucial part of conducting bomber operations worldwide. J-GSOC and 608th Air Operations Center planners coordinate with USSTRATCOM and global combatant commands (GCCs) to develop objectives and tasks for specific BTFs based on the National Defense Strategy and USSTRATCOM campaign plans.

The success of the global BTF mission set is directly linked with the tanker support received from both US Transportation Command and the different geographic combatant commands.

B-1B Systems

Details of the systems and sub-systems of the B-1B Lancer supersonic heavy bomber aircraft.

A weapons loader lowers the Launcher Load Frame in preparation for moving it to the flight-line at Dyess Air Force Base, Texas. The LLF is a piece of equipment that allows weapons loaders to pre-load munitions on a launcher, under the cover of a facility, prior to transporting the entire launcher/munition package to the flight-line for loading on the aircraft. US Air Force/Senior Airman Josiah Brown

The B-1B is designed for a speed of Mach 1-plus at altitude, and very high subsonic speeds at low levels. It also boasts intercontinental range without refuelling. Power is provided by four General Electric F101-GE-102 augmented turbofan engines each generating 30,750lb of thrust.

The aircraft has three weapons bays, with provisions in the forward bays for a movable bulkhead to increase bay length. There are structural provisions for mounting external pylons for stores or fuel tanks. The variable sweepback wings can be stopped at any angle between 15º and 67.5º.

The crew of four consists of the pilot, co-pilot, and two weapon systems operators. The crew compartment is pressurised.

ESCAPE SYSTEM

Four ACES II (Advanced Concept Ejection Seat) B-1B seats incorporating personal parachutes and emergency oxygen are used for crew ejection. The seat uses three recovery modes which are automatic functions depending on airspeed and altitude when bale out occurs. The ACES B-1B ejection seat is identical to the ACES II high technology seats installed in the A-10, F-15, and F-16 but also has armrests, comfort cushions, and limb restraints.

BAYS AND FUEL TANKS

The B-1B has five major equipment bays: one forward, one central and one aft equipment bay, and two wheel-well bays. In addition, there are four smaller bays, two called annex bays just aft of the central bay, and two called side fairing bays, one in each fuselage wing root.

There are two 15ft-long weapons bays forward of the wing-carry-through structure and one 15ft-long bay aft of the main landing gear wheel wells.

> ## "The variable sweepback wings can be stopped at any angle between 15º and 67.5º."

The two forward bays have a movable bulkhead which may be repositioned to provide two 15ft bays, one 22ft bay, plus an 8ft bay forward, or left out entirely to provide one 31ft bay. This movable bulkhead allows high payload versatility.

Fuselage, wing-carry-through, and wing outer panel tanks constitute the bulk of the fuel storage provisions.

MATERIALS

The major material used in the B-1B is aluminium. The four fuselage sections, both wings' box sections, and both nacelles are primarily aluminium reinforced with steel and titanium structural members. The main landing gear is made of steel and is structurally

> ## "The B-1B is designed to be self-sufficient and operate from remote locations with minimum or no ground support equipment."

improved to support the additional weight. The wing-carry-through structure and wing root attachment points, as well as the attach point pins, are made of titanium.

Advanced composite materials are used in the wing flap area and other areas of the aircraft. Poly Quartz is used for the nose and tail cones, and the side radar fairings.

DESIGN

The B-1B is designed to be self-sufficient and operate from remote locations with minimum or no ground support equipment.

There are two auxiliary power units (APUs) which provide on-board engine start, electrical, hydraulic, and pneumatic power, and environmental control system (ECS) cooling for certain areas on the aircraft. In addition, the APUs support all required functions for cockpit alert.

The aircraft's electrical system incorporates a central integrated test system (CITS) which lends itself to minimum manual troubleshooting and false component removals. The system provides fault detection and fault isolation. A CITS recorder provides a tape of component or system operation for playback and fault analysis.

CONFIGURATION

The aircraft has several unique features not found in aircraft of the same or larger size.

The area ruled fuselage concept is employed to prevent boundary layer air separation at high subsonic and supersonic speeds.

The blended wing body presents a clean frontal area where the wing blends into the fuselage instead of attaching to it. This concept reduces drag and additional lift is provided by the fuselage portion of the wing.

The blended wing combined with the area ruled fuselage creates a very smooth airflow across the aircraft surfaces and reduces drag significantly.

The variable sweep wings are used in the forward (extended) position for landing, take-off, and low speed flight, and the aft (sweepback) position for high-speed flight.

ENGINES

The aircraft is powered by four GE Aviation F101-GE-102 engines mounted in pairs, side by side, in nacelles attached to the lower surface of the right- and left-wing roots. Each engine is a dual spool, mixed flow, augmented turbofan in the 15,000-plus pound thrust class (un-augmented) and 30,750lb thrust class (augmented). The high-pressure section (core engine) consists of a nine-stage compressor in which the angles of the inlet guide vanes and the stator vanes of the first three compressor stages are variable, an annular combustor, and a single-stage high tip speed turbine.

A Launcher Load Frame sits alongside a B-1B Lancer prior to loading at Dyess Air Force Base, Texas. After the B-1B was deemed no longer nuclear certified, the pre-load capability went unused for 30 years until now. US Air Force/Senior Airman Josiah Brown

A weapons loader assists in the transportation of the Launcher Load Frame to the flight-line for loading at Dyess Air Force Base, Texas, Jan. 9, 2023. US Air Force/Senior Airman Josiah Brown

The turbine, turbine nozzle, and shroud are air cooled. The combustor is equipped with fuel injectors and a dual high and low energy ignition system. The low-pressure section consists of a two-stage fan with movable inlet guide vanes and a two-stage low-pressure turbine.

The augmenter system uses a sequenced fuel injection system and an automatic ignition system. The augmenter exhaust nozzle is a variable area convergent-divergent type with mechanically linked primary and secondary flaps and seals.

Air entering the engine is initially compressed by the fan which directs the flow into the core compressor and the annular fan duct on the outside of the compressor case. Air entering the core compressor is further compressed and then discharged into the combustor, where it is mixed with fuel and ignited. As combustion occurs, the expanding gas passes into the turbine section to drive the high-pressure turbine, which drives the core compressor, and the low-pressure turbines, which drive the fans.

On leaving the turbine section, the exhaust gas mixes with air from the fan duct and flows out of the exhaust nozzle. During augmented operation, additional fuel is injected into

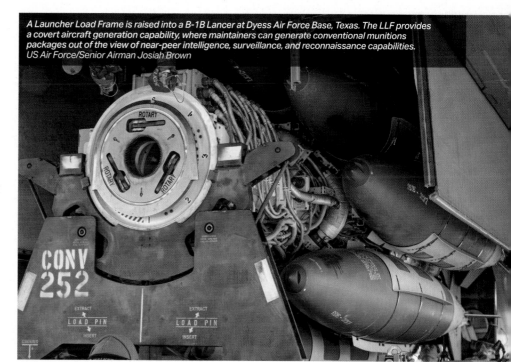

A Launcher Load Frame is raised into a B-1B Lancer at Dyess Air Force Base, Texas. The LLF provides a covert aircraft generation capability, where maintainers can generate conventional munitions packages out of the view of near-peer intelligence, surveillance, and reconnaissance capabilities. US Air Force/Senior Airman Josiah Brown

Armament systems specialists prepare to load ordnance onboard a B-1B Lancer. US Navy/Mass Communication Specialist 1st Class John Johnson

Maintainers align the B-1B Lancer main landing gear parallel brace with the side brace. US Air Force/SSgt David Owsianka

the air downstream of the turbine section and ignited. The gas from this combustion process expands through the exhaust nozzle and produces a significant thrust increase over that produced during nonaugmented operation.

Compressor third stage bleed air is used for the compressor and the turbine rotor cooling and for lubrication system pump pressurisation.

Fifth and ninth stage bleed air is used for the engine anti-icing, aircraft environmental control, and secondary pressurisation systems.

The engine has its own engine-mounted alternator, which supplies electrical power for all phases of engine operation except for pilot selected control and override signals. The engine-driven alternator provides power for: an ignition igniter; an augmenter fan temperature control for schedule computation; a torque motor actuation; a sensor excitation; and engine CITS signals. The low energy ignition system receives its power from the aircraft electrical system.

Each engine is controlled by a single throttle to produce an approximate linear thrust

increase with throttle advance. At each engine, control is accomplished by three systems: the main engine control system; the augmenter control system; and the engine fuel delivery system.

Engine motoring and starting power is provided by an auxiliary power unit (APU) in each nacelle. This unit is mechanically connected by a power transmission shaft to one engine accessory gearbox (No.2 and No.4) in each nacelle.

Each engine accessory drive gearbox mounts an air turbine starter (ATS), which supplies cranking torque to its engine when supplied with air.

Air can be supplied to the ATS by three different means: APU bleed air; engine bleed air from another operating engine; and a ground air source. The aircraft is equipped with cross bleed capability, so any operating engine can start the other three. In addition to the ATS capability. The No.2 and No.4 engines (right engine in each nacelle) may be started mechanically through a torque converter in the No.2 and No.4 accessory drive gearbox.

The engine also retains the capability of mounting an external air turbine starter

> *"The variable sweep wings are used in the forward (extended) position for landing, take-off, and low speed flight, and the aft (sweepback) position for high-speed flight."*

> ## "According to pilots, the aircraft handles more like a heavy fighter than a bomber."

aircraft by movement of the primary control surfaces. The primary control surfaces consist of a two-section rudder, four spoiler panels on the upper surface of each wing, and movable horizontal stabilisers. The pitch attitude of the aircraft is controlled by symmetrical deflection of the horizontal stabilisers' surfaces. Roll attitude is controlled by asymmetrical deflection of the horizontal stabiliser's surfaces and by deflection of the wing spoiler panels. Yaw control is accomplished by deflection of the rudders on the rear spar of the vertical stabiliser.

FLIGHT CONTROL SYSTEMS

Hydraulic servo-actuators are used to deflect the horizontal stabilisers, wing spoiler panels, and lower rudder. The upper rudder section is deflected by mechanical rotary actuators driven by two hydraulic power drive units. The pilot's and co-pilot's sticks are mechanically interconnected and are attached to hydromechanical control paths which provide both pilots mechanical control of the horizontal stabilisers and inboard spoilers for pitch and roll control. The pilot's and co-pilot's mechanically interconnected rudder pedals are attached to hydromechanical control paths to provide mechanical control of the upper rudder for yaw control. Electrical control of the horizontal stabilisers and lower rudder from the interconnected control sticks and rudder pedals is via a Stability and Control Augmentation System (SCAS).

The SCAS provides aircraft stability about all three axes at all airspeeds by transforming signals from pilot inputs and aircraft motion into flight control surface displacement to produce the

desire damping and manoeuvre control. Electrical control of the outboard spoilers from the interconnected control sticks is through a spoiler controller system that provides optimum roll control at airspeeds below Mach 1. The inboard wing spoiler panels, in addition to providing roll control augmentation, can be used as speed brakes when the aircraft is airborne.

All the spoiler panels are used as speed brakes on the ground. Separate electro-mechanical control paths to the primary surface actuators provide pitch, roll, and yaw trim functions. A trim-for-take-off system is provided to ensure that all surfaces are in the position required for take-off.

CREW COMPARTMENT FLIGHT CONTROLS

The flight controls within the crew compartment issue commands to the various surfaces for aircraft manoeuvres as dictated by the pilot or co-pilot. The controls for the most part are conventional. There are two fighter type control sticks, rather than the conventional bomber wheel and column. According to pilots, the aircraft handles more like a heavy fighter than a bomber.

The two control sticks, which are mechanically linked together, may be disengaged by a handle located on the pilot's console in the event of an emergency. There are two separate control paths for surface movement.

The pilot's stick is mechanically linked to the actuating mechanisms for direct control. The co-pilot's stick is electrically linked to the SCAS to provide a fly-by-wire system. Either of these systems will function independently of the other if the disengage mechanism is used.

through an adapter located on the bottom gear case of the engine.

Normal engine start is accomplished by mechanically cranking the right engine through the torque converting in the accessory drive gearbox and by cranking the left engine with the ATS mounted on the accessory drive gearbox with air supplied by the respective APU.

If the accessory drive gearbox is not coupled to the APU during an engine start attempt, the aircraft will automatically select the alternate start mode in which both engines in a single nacelle will be started by the air turbine starters with bleed air supplied by the APU.

Ground air can be supplied through a connection located on the bottom of each nacelle. This air will usually be supplied by a standard military ground start cart. The normal start procedure is to start one engine from the cart and the other three engines from the operating engine via the cross-bleed system.

FLIGHT CONTROLS

The primary flight control system provides pitch, roll, and yaw attitude control of the

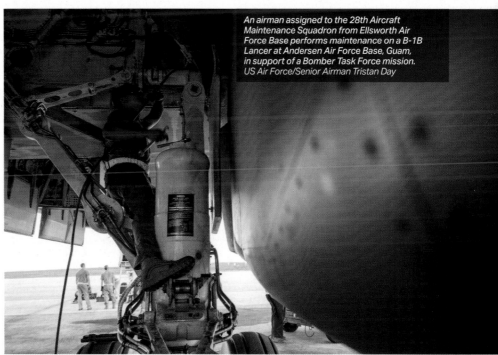

An airman assigned to the 28th Aircraft Maintenance Squadron from Ellsworth Air Force Base performs maintenance on a B-1B Lancer at Andersen Air Force Base, Guam, in support of a Bomber Task Force mission.
US Air Force/Senior Airman Tristan Day

The rudder pedals are mechanically linked together and may be moved by either the pilot or co-pilot. There is no disengage system; however, the co-pilot rudder pedals do incorporate the electrical transducers for electrical signals to the SCAS. It means that if there's a mechanical disconnect of some sort, there is still electrical control of the rudder. If the mechanical system becomes jammed for some reason, there is no rudder control. The pedals are adjustable to suit the individual crew member.

The wing sweep control handles are mechanically linked together and mechanically linked to the wing sweep control mechanism. The detents indicate to the crew command positions of wing sweep: 15° (full forward) and 20°. The wings have the capability of being stopped at any position

between 15° which is used for take-off, landing, and slow manoeuvring such as when the aircraft is required to loiter and 67.5° (full aft) which is selected for maximum speeds. A position of 25° is generally selected for cruise flight.

A flap and landing gear interlock mechanism interfaces with the crank and detent assembly to limit the wing sweep motion. With the flaps extended, the interlock prevents sweeping the wings aft beyond 20°. With the landing gear down, the interlock prevents sweeping the wing aft beyond 35°. A cross ship control shaft interconnects the control mechanism to provide control redundancy and wing position synchronisation.

There is an alternate electrical control which will sweep the wings forward or hold their position.

Mechanical feel for the crew is introduced into the controls by the installation of artificial feel bungees in the forward and aft portion of the control mechanism.

INTEGRATED BATTLE STATION
An eight-year project to install the Integrated Battle Station, or IBS, on the B-1B fleet was completed ahead of schedule in late September 2020. Sixty aircraft went through the modification process that began in late 2012.

The IBS was developed as three separate modifications: the fully integrated datalink, the vertical situational display unit, and the central integrated test system. It was the largest, most complicated modification ever performed on the B-1B and it gave the flight deck a whole new look.

> "The upgrade improves aircrew situational awareness with colour displays, and enhanced navigation and communication systems."

To complete a modification of this size took thousands of man-hours of work with 120 mechanics and support personnel assigned to the modification line working two shifts at the Oklahoma City Air Logistics Complex, during 1,050,000 hours of planned work over an eight-year period.

The completed modification enhances B-1B flight operations and gives the crews more flexibility in performing various missions with much greater battlefield awareness of surrounding threats whether air-to-air or ground-to-air and provides a much faster capability to execute both defensive and offensive manoeuvres needed in any conflict.

The upgrade improves aircrew situational awareness with colour displays, and enhanced navigation and communication systems.

LATEST SOFTWARE

In late March 2023, the 337th Test and Evaluation Squadron based at Dyess Air Force Basse, Texas completed the Field Development Evaluation (FDE) of Sustainment Block-18 (SB-18), a major software block upgrade providing new capabilities and improvements to the B-1B Lancer avionics suite.

SB-18 is the largest in both cost and scope since the Integrated Battle Station (IBS) upgrade of 2014 and includes updates to the avionics flight software, the central integrated test system, the electrical multiplexing system, graphics controller, and the tactical display subsystem.

SB-18's simplified sensor targeting enables a crew to target emerging targets of opportunity more expeditiously, bring legacy flight software functionality to the IBS interface, and improve the B-1B's organic multi-target capability. It also provides a more stable and functional storage capability for mission data and improves the defensive avionics suite's processing and integration into the IBS framework.

The 337th TES has already begun evaluating the first iteration of a new agile software construct known as Agile Software Replacement-19, which will provide more rapid upgrade fielding timelines to outfit the combat units with the most up-to-date and advanced systems. It will also streamline the acquisitions timeline to integrate new and emerging technologies into the weapons system, enabling the B-1B to provide the largest conventional payload and survive threats across all mission requirements.

Bad to the Bone

On June 29, 2023, the B-1B Lancer bomber will mark its 38th anniversary of service entry. The 28th Bomb Wing remains the primary combat-coded B-1B unit.

O n June 29, 1985, B-1B serial number 83-0065 was delivered to Dyess Air Force Base, Texas. This was the first aircraft delivered to Strategic Air Command (SAC) and was assigned to the first operational B-1B unit, the 337th Bombardment Squadron - part of the 96th Bombardment Wing. The 337th BS declared initial operational capability on October 1, 1986.

Today, B-1B 83-0065 named *Spirit of Abilene* is preserved as a static display at the Dyess Linear Air Park.

Dyess still has B-1Bs on the ramp. These days the bombers are assigned to Air Force Global Strike Command's 7th Bomb Wing in residence since October 1, 1993, the day that the wing was reactivated there following transfer from Carswell Air Force Base near Fort Worth, Texas.

SAC's second B-1B wing, the former B-52H-equipped 28th Bombardment Wing based at Ellsworth Air Force Base, South Dakota received the first of 35 Lancers in January 1987. Still resident at Ellsworth, the 28th BW continues to fly the B-1B Lancer.

Both the 7th BW and the 28th BW are assigned to Air Force Global Strike Command's 8th Air Force and operate all but a couple of the 45 B-1Bs still in service.

The 28th BW is the premier combat wing with two squadrons assigned while the 7th BW has the B-1B formal training unit and just one combat squadron.

FLYING THE B-1B

Speaking about the handling characteristics of the B-1B – colloquially known as 'the Bone' from B-One - Colonel Steve Biggs a former B-1B pilot told the author: "It's a very manoeuvrable aeroplane, handles very much like a big T-38 without the same G capability, it turns well, rolls well, and flies well in supersonic flight at low level."

Swing-wings provide various options for the pilot, and these are governed primarily by the mode of flight. The wing sweep angle is set using a manual lever - it's not automatic. "Twenty-five degrees is our typical en route cruise setting which helps to save fuel," said Col Biggs. Others are 45° for cruise at Mach 0.8 or 55° at Mach 0.9 and 67° (wings fully aft), which is selected almost exclusively for low-level, supersonic flying.

According to Biggs, the drag penalty for different wing positions varies by just a few thousand pounds of fuel per hour (7,000-10,000lb). Unsurprisingly, in supersonic flight with the wings fully aft, the fuel burn rate increases to 36,000lb per hour.

And how does the aeroplane differ in terms of handling in the different flight regimes? "When the wings are fully aft you can pull more G which allows you to make tighter turns and other high-performance manoeuvres because of the configuration of the aircraft," he said.

"Flying fast at low-level gives a different perspective, you've got the ground rush, more G, you can bank it up, you can turn it tighter, it requires more attention, you're more on edge because you're closer to the ground whereas up high it's a more benign and very different flight regime," he said.

Flown by a crew of four, a pilot, co-pilot and two weapon systems officers (WSO or wizzo), the B-1B is every bit a bomber. Interplay between the crew members is essential. The

A B-1B assigned to the 28th Bomb Wing departs Nellis Air Force Base on a night-time mission during Exercise Red Flag. Paul Ridgway

> "It's a very manoeuvrable aeroplane, handles very much like a big T-38 without the same G capability, it turns well, rolls well, and flies well in supersonic flight at low level."

pilot flying the aircraft (this can be the pilot or co-pilot) concentrates on just that. The other pilot watches a screen that shows the moving map display, or the video generated by the Sniper pod. That screen sits in the middle of the console so that both pilots can see it. "It's the pilot not flying whose job is to make sure that the whole scenario is running correctly and that the front nav station is coordinated correctly and getting the right information," said Col Biggs.

"Communication between the pilots and wizzos is all about making sure we have the right co-ordinates and the right target." Explaining how the pilots know what the WSOs are doing, Colonel Biggs told the author: "The wizzos are the ones actually loading the weapons with the correct target information, and controlling the Sniper pod, we don't control the pod from up front, we just see the video."

SNIPER POD

Upgrades to legacy aircraft are common, the most recent upgrade to the B-1B involved integration of the AAQ-33 Sniper XR advanced targeting pod. In the case of the B-1 the pod is operated by a weapon systems officer using a laptop computer.

In 2007, Lieutenant General Gary North, Commander CENTAF (Central Command Air Force) issued an urgent operational need for the AAQ-33 Sniper pod to be fitted on to the B-1B.

Because the B-1B had limitations in being able to identify targets, perform battle damage assessment, and no means to capture video or send it back to a JTAC, the request was given the highest priority. The final decision to field Sniper on the B-1B was made in the third quarter of 2007.

Developmental testing by the 419 Flight Test Squadron at Edwards Air Force Base, California, operational testing by the 337th Test and Evaluation Squadron (TES) from Dyess Air Force Base and training at Ellsworth was conducted simultaneously.

Sniper pods used on the B-1B are exclusive to the type because of the kind of video down link and associated cabling fitted. Exclusivity aided the training effort because no other units could compete to use the pods.

Despite that advantage, training with Sniper was impinged because the first squadron scheduled to deploy with the pod was well underway with its spin-up training. The 37th BS was due to deploy to Al Udeid in the summer of 2008.

With only a few aircraft fitted with the pod, the number of training sorties available was limited such that an initial cadre (mainly instructors) was trained and deployed.

So tight was the timescale that the 337th Test and Evaluation Squadron ran the operational test effort at Ellsworth to enable early training of the instructors before the pod-equipped B-1B was released for operational training. "We had exactly 55 days from our first training sortie to the first time we went into combat with the Sniper pod," said Lieutenant Colonel Kevin Kennedy, the then commander of the 34th BS.

WSOs with less experience were soon able to undertake more training on 12-hour plus missions to Afghanistan. Those with experience controlled the pod during combat, while those with less experience picked-up additional training while in transit to and from base.

It is remarkable to consider that during the 55-day period there were never more than four Sniper-equipped jets. During the period, the maintenance squadron faced significant challenges to accomplish a normal day's flying schedule. "We should have had about a dozen aircraft to fly to accomplish the training, we had four, and completed 78 sorties over the 55 days," said Colonel Thomas Fitch, then commander of the 28th Maintenance Group. "Every Sniper modified aeroplane had to be ready to fly, keeping 100% mission capability on a small pool of aeroplanes is very difficult," he added.

Integration of Sniper on to the B-1B was completed in under a year, a process that might normally take up to five years. But the modification process took longer than expected and modified B-1Bs were in short supply during the spring of 2008. When the 37th BS deployed, only two of the jets had Sniper.

A crew from the 37th Expeditionary Bomb Squadron flew the first combat sortie with a B-1B equipped with a Sniper pod on August 4, 2008.

Traditionally considered the defensive system officer, the WSO in the left seat operates the electronic counter measures systems and defends the jet against missile or other threats using chaff and flares. His or her counterpart sitting in the right seat is the offensive systems officer who loads the weapon with coordinates and, depending on the type of weapon, sets the system in auto for release.

B-1B 86-0139/EL with special tail markings for the 28th Bomb Wing commander, taxies to the runway at Ellsworth Air Force Base, South Dakota. *Paul Ridgway*

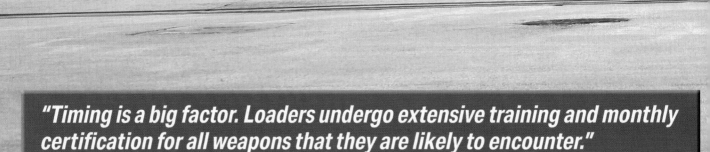

"Timing is a big factor. Loaders undergo extensive training and monthly certification for all weapons that they are likely to encounter."

Colonel Biggs explained: "For most of the GPS-guided weapons, we [the pilots] have to throw a release switch that gives consent to release the weapon from the front station.

For example, the pilot must throw the switch to give consent to release a GBU-31 JDAM when it is carried on a non-conventional rotary launcher. By contrast a GBU-38 JDAM carried on a non-CRL does not require consent."

AIRCRAFT PREPARATION
Supporting 24-hour flight operations requires continuous work to regenerate aircraft. 'Code 2' or 'code 3' write-ups are primarily what take up the time to regenerate a jet. A 'code 2' means that the aircraft is partially mission capable and might still be able to be used whereas 'code 3' means the jet will be grounded until fixed.

The aircraft has a sophisticated diagnostic system. At the end of every sortie the maintenance debrief crew must download that data and give it to the specialists who look for the flight critical issues.

The Aircraft Maintenance Squadron is also responsible for loading bombs. This is a specialised job undertaken by ammo troops called 'loaders' who despite their munitions-based role are also assigned to the maintenance squadron. Working in groups of four their task is to load each aircraft with the stores required for the mission.

The process of determining an aircraft's weapon load starts with the mission plan when operating from Ellsworth or an air tasking order (ATO) when deployed. The latter is distributed to a various organisations including legal specialists and the crew.

Once the target(s) is/are deemed to be viable, the munition or bomb with the required battlefield effect is selected and an ops order is issued 24 hours prior to the mission.

BUILDING AND LOADING JDAM
The Joint Direct Attack Munition (JDAM) weapon has proven to be an effective capability integrated on the B-1B. JDAM comprises a 500lb Mk82 or 2,000lb Mk84 iron bomb fitted with a tail kit containing an inertial navigation system/global positioning system guidance kit.

Fitted with a JDAM tail kit, a Mk82 becomes a GBU-38 and a Mk84 a GBU-31.

Ammo troops assigned to the 28th Munitions Squadron bring each of the JDAM's six components out of different storage areas and into a build pad for assembly. Each component is delivered to a specific area of

a conveyor system used to build the weapon for fitting to the bomb body. The fin (the component containing the guidance system) must be ops-checked before it can be used.

As a JDAM rolls off the conveyor system it is put onto a trailer and taken for inspection to check its assembly and fusing. Inspection complete and the trailers loaded, the bombs are taken to a staging area for delivery to the maintenance squadron within six hours.

The process from breaking out (from storage) to staging takes 68 hours. Timing is a big factor. Loaders undergo extensive training and monthly certification for all weapons that they are likely to encounter.

As an example, if the aircraft is scheduled to depart at 10:00, the maintenance squadron will prepare the aircraft by 05:00, which means the loaders require the weapons by 07:00 to have sufficient time to complete the loading process.

A pilot assigned to the 37th Expeditionary Bomber Squadron climbs aboard a B-1B Lancer for a mission from a base in southwest Asia. US Air Force/SSgt Robert Barney

Bomb loaders position a 2,000lb GBU-31 JDAM onto an MHU-40 munitions handling unit for loading into a B-1B weapons bay. US Air Force

Loaders can mix GBU-31s and GBU-38s on a CRL, although some modifications are required. Loaders can also mix GBU-31s and GBU-38s with the AGM-158 JASSM (Joint Air-to-Surface Standoff Missile) but doing so requires the launcher to be modified.

The rotary action of the CRL allows the required bomb, whether it's a GBU-31 or a GBU-38, to be moved to the release position. This procedure is undertaken by a WSO.

A JDAM carries a programmable fuse, which allows the fuse setting to be changed to minimise collateral damage and/or to maximise the weapon effect.

By comparison, the older and less frequently used conventional bomb module (CBM) will suspend and forcibly eject up to 28 stores. It incorporates two hooks in tandem with a 14in suspension capability and was typically used for 500lb-class iron bombs. A B-1B fitted with three CBMs can carry 84 bombs.

THE 28TH BOMB WING AND B-1B LANCER MIX

The 37th Bomb Squadron returned to operational duty with the 28th Bomb Wing in January 1987, just in time to join the 77th Bomb Squadron in training on the US Air Force's sleek new bomber. The first B-1B Lancer arrived at Ellsworth on January 21, 1987.

In 1989, the wing's B-1Bs earned the Fairchild Trophy, Crumm Linebacker Trophy, Eaker Trophy, and the Omaha Trophy for superior bomber operations and being the outstanding wing in Strategic Air Command.

Strategic Air Command redesignated the 28th BW as the 28th Wing on September 1, 1991, and once again assigned it directly under the 8th Air Force—and as part of the new objective wing organisation—reactivated the old 28th Bomb Group under the new name of the 28th Operations Group.

On September 28, 1991, the US secretary of defense ordered all US Air Force B-1B bombers and tankers off alert. On June 1, 1992, the 28th Wing changed its name back to the 28th Bomb Wing. On that day Strategic Air Command was inactivated and the 28th BW's new major command, Air Combat Command (ACC) was activated.

In 1993, the 28th BW's B-1Bs were the first in ACC to transition from the strategic role to an all-conventional mission. The transition meant the 28th BW's operational squadrons, the 37th and 77th BS, could be deployed anywhere in the world to meet national defence needs.

Three 500lb GBU-38 JDAMs loaded on a conventional rotary launcher, also known as a LAU-144/A Munitions Launcher Assembly, inside a B-1B weapons bay. US Air Force

When the loaders receive the weapons their first job is to verify that the bombs match the ops order. Assuming there are no issues, they then re-check settings on the specific munitions. Prior to receiving any weapons, the loaders must check that the aircraft is fitted with the correct launchers to hold the bombs.

GBU-31 and GBU-38 JDAMs are carried on a conventional rotary launcher (CRL) also known as a LAU-144/A Munitions Launcher Assembly (MLA). Measuring 15ft in length, a B-1B can carry a single CRL in each of its three weapon bays.

Each CRL incorporates eight BRU-56/A racks with two hooks in tandem with a 30in suspension capability, each rack suspends and releases one store, and provides electrical, mechanical, and pneumatic interface between the aircraft and the stores.

Over 120,000 pounds of thrust powers B-1B 86-0095/EL into the Nevada sky on a mission flown as part of Exercise Red Flag. Paul Ridgway

BONE 23

In the early hours of July 13, 2008, elements of a Combined Joint Task Force (CJTF), alongside Afghanistan National Army soldiers, came under heavy fire while defending Vehicle Patrol Base Wanat in Afghanistan's Waygul Valley, east of Kabul.

After the dust had settled from the assault, it was described by the US Central Command's Deputy Combined Forces Air Component Commander (DCFACC), Major General Douglas Raaberg, as "the largest co-ordinated attack by Anti-Afghan Forces [AAF] in over three years." Subsequent CJTF investigations estimated an enemy force of over 200. During the initial onslaught, a US observation post was overrun resulting in nine friendly casualties. Faced with an overwhelming force, the US ground forces called for immediate air support and the crew of Bone 23 was first on the scene. Major Norman, an instructor pilot with the 37th Expeditionary Bomb Squadron 'Tigers', was mission lead and aircraft commander. His crew included: Lieutenant Boyd (pilot) as well as Captain Kaylene and Captain Louis (WSOs).

At the time they were requested, Bone 23 was five hours into a planned 12-hour mission, carrying a standard load of 20 GPS-guided munitions, and preparing to aerial refuel. Understanding the desperate ground situation, and despite the low fuel state, the crew responded urgently.

En route, Maj Norman co-ordinated with the Air Support Operations Center (ASOC) to move air-refuelling tankers as near as possible to the location.

Lt Boyd took the aircraft to its maximum performance ceiling to ensure a speedy strike and configured the radios to contact the Joint Terminal Attack Controller (JTAC).

Capt Kaylene surveyed the area of the troops in contact (TIC) with the aircraft's synthetic aperture radar in preparation for weapons employment. Capt Louis struggled to establish radio communication with the JTAC but did make contact and received a situation update. Weak radios and sheer terrain around the outpost hampered the crew's ability to communicate with the troops under fire.

Aware that the Waygul Valley was one of the steepest in the area, Maj Norman directed a tight orbit, while Lt Boyd and Capt Kaylene used onboard mission planning tools to analyse terrain and determine the best locations in which to maintain contact with the JTAC. With only 20 minutes of loiter time before fuel ran out, Lt Boyd minimised fuel flow while maintaining the required airspeed and altitude for weapons delivery; holding the jet in a steep bank over the valley to maximise communications.

As Capt Louis calmly assured the JTAC that Bone 23 was on station and ready for immediate nine-line tasking, the JTAC relayed that his position was under sustained heavy machine-gun and rocket-propelled grenade fire.

The JTAC asked for an immediate attack with a 2,000lb GBU-31 on the most lethal enemy firing position, only 820ft east of the nearest friendly position. Recognising a 'Danger Close' situation that would require further detailed co-ordination, Maj Norman recommended a 500lb GBU-38 JDAM to reduce the potential for fratricide.

The crew immediately compared their radar presentation with onboard satellite imagery and correlated them with the JTAC's verbal description of the area; this enabled the crew to quickly complete mandatory crosschecks confirming appropriate co-ordinates for the weapon and minimising the risk to friendly forces.

Under intense pressure to deliver weapons as quickly as possible, with tension heightened by the sound of heavy gunfire over the radio, Capt Kaylene deftly applied the special instructions for weapons employment, while entering target co-ordinates into a GBU-38. The co-ordinates were verified by the crew and read back to the JTAC for confirmation – within minutes of arriving on the scene, the crew was poised to strike its first target.

As Bone 23 turned in for the first attack, a two-ship of F-15E Strike Eagles checked in to support the same TIC. As the on-scene airborne commander, Maj Norman co-ordinated airspace and weapon release de-confliction by directing the F-15E formation to stay west of the Waygul Valley, while Bone 23 prosecuted the enemy position. Lt Boyd guided the aircraft to meet weapon parameters with less than 45 seconds before release. The crew confirmed the final targeting solution, the JTAC declared 'Cleared hot' and one minute later, less than 15 minutes after Bone 23's arrival on station, the 500lb JDAM impacted the target and JTAC shouted 'Good hit!'

Lt Boyd manoeuvred the B-1 left, off target, to set up for an immediate re-attack. Maj Norman considered the jet's fuel status and the overcast weather that would preclude the F-15Es from employing laser-guided weapons and limited them to only JDAM attacks. With the JTAC requesting an immediate re-attack on the same position and just minutes until they would need fuel, Maj Norman requested the tanker move overhead the flight, affording 10 additional minutes before refuelling. A coordinated handoff to the F-15Es would have significantly delayed the release of the next weapon.

Given the dire situation on the ground, the crew of Bone 23 elected to stay as long as possible – seconds after the first impact, additional Anti-Afghan Forces (AAF) reoccupied the original enemy position and resumed their fire.

With the aircraft postured to re-attack, Bone 23's WSOs quickly reassigned two more GBU-38s and co-ordinated with the JTAC to strike the target just five minutes after the first impact. After the two hits, lethal fire from that position stopped immediately and did not resume.

The enemy was now pursuing the attack from another firing position, and the JTAC still needed air support. Knowing he would have to depart immediately for refuelling following the second bomb run, Major Norman provided a handover to the F-15E formation with his crew's third 'nine-line' target tasking.

He estimated Bone 23 would be away for 20 minutes to refuel and expected the F-15E flight to have released all their JDAMs during that time. It meant the B-1B could return from the tanker with sufficient fuel to enable more than three hours of coverage time and with 16 precision-guided weapons remaining, to support Task Force Rock.

At this point, any further delay in refuelling would force Maj Norman to divert to an airfield in Afghanistan where his aircraft would become a target for indirect fire. The crew of Bone 23 worked to build a third targeting solution, while minimising fuel use and continuously recalculating the minimum amount of fuel required to divert the aircraft to an airfield in Afghanistan.

After a target update and the completion of required crosschecks by the WSOs, Lt Boyd performed an aggressive manoeuvre to achieve weapon release airspeed just before clearance from the JTAC. Nine minutes after receipt of their third 'nine-line' targeting message, the JTAC again reported 'Good hit!'.

Within 30 minutes of radio contact with the JTAC, Bone 23 had executed three bomb runs, releasing four GBU-38s on two key AAF firing positions before departing the area just below 'Bingo' fuel to join the tanker.

Co-ordinating for immediate refuelling priority, the crew of Bone 23 vectored the tanker to ensure an expeditious rendezvous, and Maj Norman uploaded 60,000lb of fuel in 10 minutes. This prevented the need to divert and enabled the crew to return to the task of supporting the JTAC. During refuelling, Capt Louis maintained radio contact with the troops at VPB Wanat.

Despite Bone 23's readiness to roll in again, the Air Support Operations Center informed the crew that ground alert A-10s were en route to support the VPB Wanat TIC because they were needed to deal with another situation in the remote far western part of Afghanistan, one that was well beyond the range of all other available air assets.

Bone 23 supported this follow-on TIC successfully and flew the rest of its scheduled close air support period uneventfully, returning to the forward operating base hours later.

On landing, Major General Raaberg met with the crew to thank them for their outstanding support of the JTAC and the ground forces at VPB Wanat in the face of a well-orchestrated, complex attack, by an overwhelming force.

The crew of Bone 23 had provided the timely, precise, and ultimately 'decisive' aerial firepower needed to halt the enemy's advance and changed a potential disaster into a coalition victory.

Significantly, several wounded VPB Wanat paratroopers, who were passing through the B-1 Forward Operating Location went out of their way to show their appreciation to the crew – who, in their own words, 'saved our asses'!

According to the CJTF investigation of the VPB Wanat attack, enemy forces mounted a complex multi-axis assault that was certain to overrun the small outpost. Effective aerial firing by Bone 23 and subsequent flights stopped the enemy onslaught, making it possible to rescue a surviving US paratrooper who was cut off during the first attack. It also reduced the volume of enemy fire to the point that four wounded soldiers could be extracted by Medevac helicopter to a nearby staging area.

Post battle analysis revealed that up to 52 AAF insurgents were killed and approximately 45 wounded, primarily attributed to airpower, and specifically the crew of Bone 23.

The crew of Bone 23 won the 2008 MacKay Trophy for its action in support of the troops in Afghanistan. Administered by the United States National Aeronautic Association, the trophy is awarded by the US Air Force for the most meritorious air force flight of the year.

DOOLITTLE RAIDERS

In 1942, Lieutenant Colonel James Doolittle led 16 B-25 Mitchell bombers on the first US air raid on Japan. The air crews selected for the raid were drawn from all four squadrons assigned to the 17th Bombardment Group (Medium) based at Lexington County Airport in South Carolina. These were the 34th, 37th and 95th Bombardment Squadron (Medium) and the 89th Reconnaissance Squadron (Medium). In 2023, three of these squadrons remain on active-duty service. In its current role, the 95th Reconnaissance Squadron, a component of the 55th Operations Group based at Offutt AFB, Nebraska, is based at RAF Mildenhall in the UK. It hosts RC-135 Rivet Joint aircraft for european operations. The 34th and 37th Bomb Squadrons operate the B-1B Lancer with the 28th Bomb Wing at Ellsworth. In October 2001, B-1Bs from Ellsworth conducted some of the first attacks against Taliban targets in Afghanistan.

On April 18, 2009, the official Doolittle Raider crest, which reads 'Toujours au Danger', or 'Always into Danger' was officially passed to the aircrew from the 34th Bomb Squadron at the 67th reunion held at Columbia Metro Airport in South Carolina.

An AAQ-33 Sniper targeting pod mounted on the right side forward fuselage pylon of a B-1B Lancer. US Air Force

A B-1B Lancer awaits a pre-flight inspection at Ellsworth Air Force Base during Exercise Badlands Express in preparation for an operational readiness inspection. US Air Force/ Senior Airman Michael Keller

Phase maintenance underway on a B-1B's F101-GE-102 engine at Ellsworth Air Force Base. Paul Ridgway

> ## "The Joint Direct Attack Munition (JDAM) weapon has proven to be an effective capability integrated on the B-1B."

The concept was tested in 1993 and in early 1994 during events such as Exercise Team Spirit when B-1Bs landed in the Republic of Korea for the first time; Exercise Global Power when Ellsworth-based B-1Bs flew various long-duration, round trip sorties to release bombs at training ranges on another continent; and Exercise Bright Star when the B-1B participated for the first time in this major Joint Chiefs of Staff exercise in southwest Asia.

Between June and December 1994, 28th BW B-1Bs participated in a congressionally directed operational readiness assessment known as Dakota Challenge. The test, conducted exclusively by the 28th BW, proved the B-1B to be a versatile and reliable weapon system.

On March 31, 1995, the 77th BS, a unit that had served under the wing since 1948, inactivated. Its B-1Bs became part of ACC's reconstitution reserve. This action freed funds to allow the US Air Force to develop new precision-guided munitions. The 77th BS was not gone for long, because on April 1, 1997, the squadron was reactivated under the 28th BW and subsequently received the first B-1B aircraft upgraded to Block D configuration

in November 1988. The Block D upgrade included the integration of the GPS-guided Joint Direct Attack Munition (JDAM).

In December 1998, the 28th BW deployed B-1B aircraft under the flag of the 28th Air Expeditionary Group in support of Operation Desert Fox and undertook two combat missions and employed the first bombs dropped by a B-1B on an enemy target.

In March 1999, the 28th BW became a lead unit for the Expeditionary Air Force concept, which represented a fundamental change in the way the US Air Force would fight wars. Expeditionary Aerospace Forces would respond quickly to worldwide crises while reducing the operations tempo for personnel.

Concurrently, the 28th BW deployed five B-1B aircraft to RAF Fairford, UK in support of Operation Allied Force, NATO's air campaign launched to halt the humanitarian catastrophe unfolding in Kosovo; the B-1Bs struck the first Serbian military targets in Kosovo on April 1, 1999. By the end of the air campaign on June 10, 1999, Ellsworth B-1Bs had flown 100 combat missions.

Between September and November 1999, Cairo West Air Base in Egypt was the temporary home to three B-1B aircraft and

DOOLITTLE'S RAID

On April 18, 1942, Americans retaliated for the Japanese attack on Pearl Harbor. While nervous sailors watched, 16 B-25 Mitchell medium bombers with five-man crews took off, one after another, from the wooden deck of the aircraft carrier USS Hornet (CV 8).

Beginning with the lead bomber piloted by Lt Col James 'Jimmy' Doolittle, each B-25 roared down the carrier deck, plunged briefly from view as if to collide with the wave tops, and then reappeared in a slow, deliberate climb. Powered by two-1,700hp Wright R-260071 radial piston engines – straining to overcome gravity at maximum weight, flying a little sluggishly - the 27,100lb (12,290kg) bombers pulled skyward setting course for Japan.

The architect of the daring attack from a naval task force deep in unfriendly waters was the short, mild-tempered Doolittle. He was a pioneer in instrument flying, navigation techniques and air racing. He would later command the Eighth Air Force, the largest formation ever assembled to do battle in the air. President Franklin D Roosevelt gave the task to Doolittle despite the objection of more experienced officers and Doolittle assembled his force – the Doolittle Raiders. In trials near Eglin Army Air Field, Florida, the raiders proved that the powerful, twin-engine B-25 could take off in less than 500ft.

When Hornet and her task force sailed far into the western Pacific, a Japanese vessel sighted the carrier. Doolittle's men were forced to take off far short of their intended launch point, a full 800 miles from the Japanese coast. "There was a lot of scrambling around," said Aviation Technician Joe Evon, an SBD Dauntless gunner whose own aircraft was stowed below decks. "As we watched them prepare to get into the air, we all felt that they must know what they were doing, or we wouldn't be here."

The B-25s zoomed up to 1,500ft, split up, and pressed separate attacks on Tokyo, Kanegawa, Kobe, Nagoya, Osaka, Yokohama, and the Yokosuka navy yard.

The mere act of getting into the sky was an extraordinary feat. In his book Thirty Seconds Over Tokyo Captain Ted Lawson described the procedure for take-off: "If a motor quit or caught fire, if a tyre went flat, if the right wing badly scraped the island [the raised structure on the carrier deck], if the left wheel went over the edge, we were to get out as quickly as we could and help the navy shove our $150,000 plane overboard. It must not, under any circumstances, be permitted to block traffic. There would be no other way to clear the forward deck for the other planes to take off."

The American public, following the war in the Pacific, was seeing newspaper headlines that told only of defeat after defeat – of the American fleet being smashed at Pearl Harbor and US troops being routed in the Philippines, overrun on Java, overwhelmed on Wake Island. Few Americans alive today remember how it felt to be beaten badly by a militarily superior foe – or the extent to which American sentiment required payback.

All 16 B-25s got aloft, navigated the western Pacific, and reached their targets. American doctrine favoured precision bombing and the Doolittle raiders felt they put their bombs in the right places. Japanese fighters engaged one or two of the Mitchells. All encountered anti-aircraft fire.

The symbolism of an assault on the Japanese homeland was more important than the damage Doolittle's B-25 crews inflicted. The attacks forced Japan to withdraw a carrier group from the Indian Ocean to defend the homeland. The Doolittle raid prompted a series of decisions in Tokyo that led to the battle of Midway – Japan's first major defeat.

Except for a crew interned in Russia, the men had to bale out – some over Japanese-held areas of China. "We ran out of fuel and had to bail out in Japanese-occupied territory," said B-25 co-pilot Robert Hite, then a second Lieutenant who retired as a Lieutenant Colonel. A wartime Japanese photograph shows Hite, blindfolded, bound, wearing a fleece-lined flight jacket and wheel hat, being escorted by Japanese guards.

He was one of the lucky ones. In all, 11 B-25 crewmen were killed or captured. The Japanese shot and killed three captured Doolittle raiders. A fourth died of malnutrition while in captivity.

Still, the entire crews of 13 of the 16 medium bombers, and all but one member of the 14th, recovered in friendly territory and returned to the United States.

In later years, surviving Doolittle raiders held reunions and established a tradition of raising silver goblets – 80 altogether, one for each crewmember – to toast their fallen comrades. In 2008, when only eight were able to attend a reunion, they decided to retire the goblets, each inscribed with a raider's name. All are now on public display at the National Museum of the Air Force in Dayton, Ohio.

Navigator Chase Nielson, also a second Lieutenant at the time of the raid who retired as a Lieutenant Colonel, and one of Hite's fellow prisoners of war, said of the Doolittle raid: "I learned… how to appreciate mankind, our democracy, and the beautiful, wonderful world we live in."

Doolittle himself never held the rank of colonel. When Roosevelt presented him with the Medal of Honor for the Tokyo attack, the president promoted Doolittle from Lieutenant Colonel to Brigadier General. Hornet was lost in waters near Guadalcanal in late 1942, but the B-25 Mitchell went on to become one of the most successful bombers of World War Two.

A B-1B Lancer uploads fuel from a KC-10A Extender. US Air Force

over 400 personnel assigned to the 28th BW in support of Exercise Bright Star. Staged by US Central Command, Bright Star was a combined-coalition exercise involving the armed forces of ten other nations.

After the terrorist attacks on the United States on September 11, 2001, the team from Ellsworth deployed several B-1B aircraft to the British Indian Ocean Territory of Diego Garcia in support of Operation Enduring Freedom. Aircraft assigned to the 37th BS based at Ellsworth and others assigned to the 34th BS based at Mountain Home Air Force Base, Idaho, formed the 28th Expeditionary Bomb Squadron.

During its deployment, the 28th EBS dropped 2,974 JDAMs, 1,471 Mk82, 135 Mk84, and 70 CBU-87 bombs: 39% of the total tonnage of bombs, which was a greater share than any other platform. The 28th EBS mission effectiveness was greater than 95% and represented 5% of the total strike aircraft missions.

Due to a drawdown in the number of B-1B aircraft in the inventory, the 77th BS at Ellsworth was inactivated and on September 19, 2002 the 34th BS moved from Mountain Home to take its place.

In preparation for Operation Iraqi Freedom, the Ellsworth-based 34th and 37th Bomb Squadrons deployed to undisclosed locations in southwest Asia. From the outset of the operation, the B-1B bombers participated in high-tempo operations over Iraq in support of ground operations.

On March 30, 2011, B-1B Lancers touched down on the runway at Ellsworth after completing the first-ever operational B-1B global strike mission launched from the United States as part of Operation Odyssey Dawn. The crews launched from Ellsworth, struck targets in Libya, landed at a forward operating location, where their aircraft were refuelled and rearmed, and hit additional targets in Libya on the return trip to Ellsworth. This was all accomplished with the same crew members.

Airmen assigned to the 28th Maintenance Group work to keep a B-1B Lancer functional at Ellsworth Air Force Base despite the extreme cold and large snowfall in the South Dakota climate. *US Air Force/Airman 1st Class Corey Hook*

Two B-1B Lancers parked on a snowy and frozen flight line at Ellsworth Air Force. *US Air Force/Airman 1st Class Corey Hook*

Airmen assigned to the 28th Maintenance Group push an oxygen cart through snow to prepare a B-1B Lancer for a mission from Ellsworth Air Force Base. *US Air Force/Airman 1st Class Corey Hook*

A B-1B Lancer assigned to the 28th Bomb Wing takes off from Nellis Air Force Base, Nevada on March 23, 2023, during Exercise Red Flag-Nellis 23-2. US Air Force/William Lewis

B-1B LANCER UNITS IN JUNE 1990
STRATEGIC AIR COMMAND

Dyess Air Force Base, Texas
15th Air Force
96th Bombardment Wing
337th Bombardment Squadron
The 96th Bombardment Wing and the 337th BS were inactivated on October 1, 1993
The first B-1B arrived at Dyess AFB on June 29, 1985.

Ellsworth Air Force Base, South Dakota
12th Air Division
28th Bombardment Wing
37th Bombardment Squadron
77th Bombardment Squadron
The 28th Bombardment Wing was redesignated as the 28th Wing on September 1, 1991 (the 37th and the 77th became Bomb Squadrons) and then as the 28th Bomb Wing on June 1, 1992. The 77th Bomb Squadron was inactivated on March 31, 1995.
The first B-1B arrived at Ellsworth in January 1987.

Grand Forks Air Force Base, North Dakota
42nd Air Division
319th Bombardment Wing
46th Bombardment Squadron
The 319th Bombardment Wing was redesignated as the 319th Wing on September 1, 1991 (the

46th became a Bomb Squadron) and then to 319th Bomb Wing on June 1, 1992. It was inactivated July 19, 1994, with the 46th BS.
The first B-1B arrived at Grand Forks in October 1987.

McConnell Air Force Base, Kansas
19th Air Division
384th Bombardment Wing
28th Bombardment Squadron
The 384th Bombardment Wing was redesignated as the 384th Wing on September 1, 1991, and inactivated on October 1, 1994. Similarly, the 28th Bombardment Squadron was redesignated as the 28th Bomb Squadron on September 1, 1991, and reassigned to the 7th Wing at Dyess AFB on October 1, 1994.
The first B-1B arrived at McConnell on January 4, 1988.

Air Force Systems Command
Edwards Air Force Base, California
6510th Test Wing
6519th Test Squadron
The 6510th Test Wing and the 6519th Test Squadron were redesignated as the 412th Test Wing and 419th Test Squadron on October 2, 1992. The 419th was redesignated as the 419th Flight Test Squadron on March 1, 1994.

> "The last of the remaining 45 B-1B aircraft is expected to serve until 2033 by when the fleet is expected to have been replaced by the B-21 Raider."

It was the first time B-1B aircraft had launched from a continental US location in support of combat operations. Conditions at the time of their launch were adverse with a temperature of 35oF and freezing fog. The bombers arrived in the Libya area of operations 12 hours after take-off, it was the deepest strike made into Libya during Operation Odyssey Dawn and kept the aircraft in hostile airspace for over 90 minutes. Post-strike, the aircraft landed at a forward operating location from where the aircrews launched a second mission within 24 hours.

A B-1B Lancer assigned to the 37th Bomb Squadron taxies to the runway at Ellsworth Air Force Base ahead of a Bomber Task Force deployment to Andersen Air Force Base, Guam on July 16, 2020. US Air Force/Airman 1st Class Quentin Marx

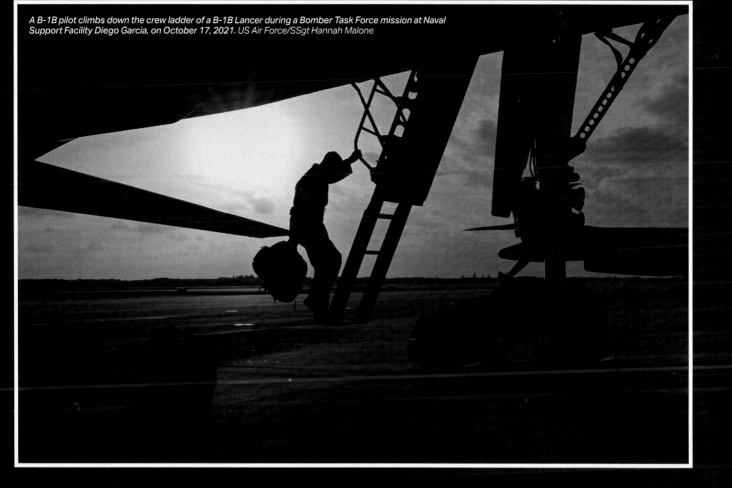

A B-1B pilot climbs down the crew ladder of a B-1B Lancer during a Bomber Task Force mission at Naval Support Facility Diego Garcia, on October 17, 2021. US Air Force/SSgt Hannah Malone

Nearly 100 targets were hit during the two-day sortie.

Two B-1B aircrews flew a 30-hour, non-stop, long-range precision strike training mission from Ellsworth to targets on a range near Guam before landing back on base as part of a Global Power training mission, on May 13-14, 2014.

The sortie tested the capabilities of 28th BW airmen to successfully load munitions, launch aircraft, effectively employ training munitions, and return to base.

On May 11, 2020, B-1B Lancers assigned to the 28th BW conducted a long-range Bomber Task Force mission in the European theatre.

During the nearly 24-hour, non-stop mission, the bombers covered over 9,400 nautical miles and included integration and interoperability training with Danish F-16s, and Polish F-16s and MiG-29s. This was the fourth such mission flown by Ellsworth-based B-1B aircrews in four weeks that included operations in the Pacific and European theatres.

A subsequent and similar mission was flown by two B-1Bs to the Black Sea region on May 29, 2020, to conduct training with the Long-Range Anti-Ship Missile. In 2018, Air Force Global Strike Command authorised Ellsworth to be the early operational capacity basing location for the AGM-158C LRASM which made the B-1B and the 28th BW the first type and unit to train and qualify on the LRASM.

On November 22, 2022, four B-1B bombers and 200 airmen assigned to the 28th BW returned to Ellsworth after a Bomber Task Force mission at Andersen Air Force Base, Guam. During the mission, the 37th Expeditionary Bomb Squadron flew 26 sorties, accruing 363 hours of flight, and integrated with the armed services of Australia, Canada, Japan, and the Republic of South Korea.

OPERATIONS

There's no doubting the enormity of the B-1B's mission - to deliver decisive combat power.

A crew chief assigned to the 37th Aircraft Maintenance Squadron marshals a B-1B Lancer onto the apron on return from a Bomber Task Force Mission at Ellsworth Air Force Base on April 7, 2021. US Air Force/Airman 1st Class Quentin Marx

Originally designed for and deployed as a low-level penetration nuclear bomber, the B-1B's role has changed. In the mid-1990s the nuclear mission was taken away and the B-1B adopted conventional roles and consequently the B-1B force has been regularly deployed since October 2001.

During combat over Afghanistan the B-1B provided a persistent presence over the battlefield, usually with one aircraft airborne, either transiting into or out of Afghanistan, driving 24-hour operations, with sorties lasting 12 hours on average. Despite the commitment to the fight in Afghanistan, the B-1 force had the capability to undertake split ops (operate from two locations at the same time) if called to deploy somewhere else in the world.

Statistics available for 2008 show how busy the Ellsworth-based B-1B squadrons were during their deployments to the US Central Command area of operations.

The 37th BS flew 566 combat missions, 6,468 combat hours and released 959 weapons, while the 34th BS flew 550 combat missions, 6,592 combat hours and released 325 weapons. Furthermore, during 2008 nine fighter units deployed to Afghanistan and released 1,089 precision-guided munitions between them. By comparison B-1Bs dropped 1,202.

To keep the long-range strike capability and the persistence of loiter, modernisation was required. The US Air Force undertook the Integrated Battle Station upgrade to 62 B-1B aircraft (the entire fleet) over an eight-year period which completed in late September 2020 at a cost of $1.25bn. The upgrade modernised the aircraft's centre integrated test system, installed a Link 16 data link, and a vertical situational display unit, requiring 17,000 parts, and 13 miles of new wiring.

Air Force Global Strike Command subsequently retired 17 B-1B bombers from its inventory, the last of which departed Edwards Air Force Base, California bound for the 309th Aerospace Maintenance and Regeneration Group at Davis-Monthan Air Force Base, Arizona on September 23, 2021.

Divestment of the 17 B-1B bombers was aligned to the US Air Force's ongoing effort to modernise its bomber fleet.

The 62-aircraft fleet had provided on-call air support to coalition troops in Afghanistan and Iraq for years and were worn-out by the operational tempo. Issues included structural fatigue at the wing-pivot points, caused by flying high and slow with the wings forward vs low and fast with the wings swept. The last of the remaining 45 B-1B aircraft is expected to serve until 2033 by when the fleet is expected to have been replaced by the B-21 Raider.

Despite its consumption of a lot of time, fuel, and money to keep them in the air, there can be no doubt that this power-laden bomber, built at Palmdale, California in the Mojave Desert, continues to serve the United States extremely well.

B-1B Lancers assigned to the 37th Expeditionary Bomb Squadron taxi to the runway ahead of a Bomber Task Force Mission at Andersen Air Force Base, Guam, on October 24, 2022. US Air Force/ Senior Airman Yosselin Campos

Airmen assigned to the 28th Bomb Wing prepare for a Bomber Task Force mission at Andersen Air Force Base, Guam, on October 24, 2022.
US Air Force/Senior Airman Yosselin Campos

Long-Range Strike

David Isby and Mark Ayton detail America's billion-dollar bomber and its operations with the 509th Bomb Wing based at Whiteman Air Force Base, Missouri.

A B-2 Spirit at Royal Australian Air Force Base Amberley, Australia on July 10, 2022, during a Bomber Task Force deployment. US Air Force/TSgt Dylan Nuckolls

Publicly unveiled at Air Force Plant 42 near Palmdale, California in November 1988, the B-2 first flew in July 1989 and entered service in December 1993.

Northrop Grumman's Block 30 B-2 Spirit stealth bomber is like no other aircraft. A tailless flying wing, its design offers both low observable stealth and high aerodynamic efficiency for long-range missions carrying munition payloads of up to 60,000lb. The ordnance is carried in two weapons bays housed within its blended fuselage and wing.

It is the only penetrating bomber in USAF service armed with nuclear gravity bombs and it will continue to be so until its replacement by a new Northrop Grumman stealth bomber, the B-21 Raider which is due to come on line in the early 2030s.

Combat employment requires the stealth bomber to strike high-value targets anywhere in the world, and return to Whiteman Air Force Base, Missouri, or recover to specific forward operating locations.

The B-2 force is normally maintained at readiness as America's silver bullet, able to penetrate hostile airspace against the highest value targets, where it can accurately deliver conventional or, if required, nuclear weapons.

The Spirit first saw combat over Kosovo in March 1999. Since then, the bombers have flown more than 3,000 combat hours that included a record-breaking 44.3-hour mission flown against targets in Afghanistan. The bomber's most recent combat missions were conducted in January 2017 against targets in Libya. The long-range B-2 has an unrefuelled

A KC-135 Stratotanker from Altus Air Force Base, Oklahoma, refuels a B-2 Spirit Stealth Bomber from Whiteman AFB during a refuelling training mission, August 29, 2012. US Air Force/Airman Franklin Ramos

"The B-2 force is normally maintained at readiness as America's silver bullet."

range of 5,200nm but with a single aerial refuelling, the Spirit can fly 8,600nm.

Development of the low-observable B-2 began in November 1981, when Northrop received a $7.3bn contract to design the Advanced Technology Bomber (ATB). Plans originally called for a fleet of 132 aircraft but only 21 were delivered when production ended.

The Spirits were initially delivered in Block 10 configuration with a combat payload limited to 2,000lb Mk84 conventional bombs or gravity nuclear weapons. Progressive upgrades saw the Block 20 variant that

featured the interim capability to deliver the GBU-37 GPS-Aided Munition. Full capability was fielded with the Block 30 configuration, which gained additional radar modes and enhanced terrain-following capability. The Block 30's weapons capabilities included the Joint Direct Attack Munition (JDAM) series and the AGM-158 Joint Stand-Off Weapon. The current Block 30 B-2A can carry as many as 80 500lb GBU-38 JDAMs.

A series of incremental upgrades have provided the B-2 with new communications systems, upgraded radar, and additional weapons including the 30,000lb bunker

busting GBU-57 Massive Ordnance Penetrator. In its nuclear penetrator role, the B-2 will carry the precision-guided B61-12 (LEP) nuclear bomb.

Flight tests with the upgraded nuclear weapon began in June 2018. Operational testing of the B61-12, which consolidates four legacy B61 variants (Mod 3, Mod 4, Mod 7, and Mod 10) into a single variant, continues. Further weapons upgrades will incorporate the capability to simultaneously carry a rotary launcher and a smart bomb rack assembly.

The US Air Force reduced the scope of the B-2's Defensive Management

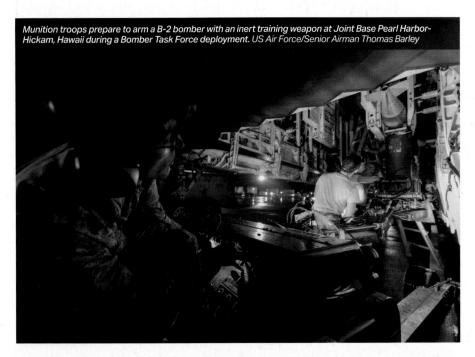

Munition troops prepare to arm a B-2 bomber with an inert training weapon at Joint Base Pearl Harbor-Hickam, Hawaii during a Bomber Task Force deployment. US Air Force/Senior Airman Thomas Barley

System — Modernized, dubbed DMS-M, which has suffered from major delays. The DMS-M/displays programme will provide the bomber with updated receiver-processors, antennas and display system that will improve aircrew situational awareness and aircraft survivability. The $3bn upgrade's development was previously extended to mid-2022 and the upgraded bomber is expected to achieve initial operational compatibility in late 2024.

The US Air Force's 20 remaining B-2 bombers (one crashed on take-off in 2008) are flown by seven test, training and operational squadrons that include a single Air National Guard associate unit – Missouri Air National Guard's 131st Bomb Wing. A single aircraft serves as a dedicated test asset at Edwards Air Force Base, California. Under current plans the B-2s will be retired no later than 2032.

CURRENT FLEET, CURRENT CONFIGURATION
Based at Whiteman Air Force Base, Missouri, the B-2 equips the active-duty 509th Bomb Wing and Missouri Air National Guard's associated 131st Bomb Wing. It remains America's most advanced strategic bomber,

A B-2 bomber being prepared for a training mission at Joint Base Pearl Harbor-Hickam, Hawaii. US Air Force/Senior Airman Thomas Barley

B-2 SPIRIT OPERATORS

Squadron	Location	Wing	Command	Code
13th Bomb Squadron (FTU)	Whiteman Air Force Base, Missouri	509th Bomb Wing	Air Force Global Strike Command	WM
31st Test and Evaluation Squadron (see Note 1)	Edwards Air Force Base, California	53rd Wing	Air Combat Command	
72nd Test and Evaluation Squadron (see Note 1)	Whiteman Air Force Base, Missouri	53rd Wing	Air Combat Command	WM
325th Weapons Squadron (see Note 1)	Whiteman Air Force Base, Missouri	53rd Wing	Air Combat Command	WM
393rd BS	Whiteman Air Force Base, Missouri	509th Bomb Wing	Air Force Global Strike Command	WM
419th FLTS	Edwards Air Force Base, California	412th Test Wing	Air Force Global Strike Command	
110th BS (see Note 2)	Whiteman Air Force Base, Missouri	Air Force Global Strike Command	Air Force Global Strike Command	WM

1. Squadron uses the aircraft assigned to the 412th Test Wing.
2. Classic associate squadron uses aircraft assigned to the 509th BW.

despite its first flight over 30 years ago on July 17, 1989, and an average airframe age of 25 years. It incorporates older, second-generation stealth technology, which is less effective than the latest, and more significantly, imposes high sustainment costs than those of more recent stealth aircraft such as the F-22 Raptor and F-35A Lightning II.

According to FY2023 figures, a B-2 costs $150,700 per-hour flight. In recent years, B-2 pilots – over 100 are based at Whiteman – fly most of their time in a simulator, and 100 hours per year in real aircraft.

Contributing to the $150,700 per-hour flight operational cost is the small size of the B-2 force, and the difficulty of sourcing needed parts from the industrial base.

Of the 20 B-2s in existence, 15 are operational, one, *Spirit of New York* is under repair after the aircraft sustained damage at Whiteman Air Force Base on December 10, 2022: the remainder are in programme depot maintenance in Air Force Plant 42 at Palmdale, California.

In June 2020, B-2 93-1087 *Spirit of Pennsylvania* became the B-2 test aircraft

B-2 PILOT INITIAL QUALIFICATION TRAINING

In 2018, the Whiteman-based 394th Combat Training Squadron was inactivated, and its training missions were transferred to the 13th Bomb Squadron. All pilots selected for the B-2 are assigned to the 13th Bomb Squadron for Initial Qualification Training flying the T-38 Talon before they fly the B-2.

Explaining, a 509th BW spokesperson said: "Whiteman's T-38 Companion Trainer Program [CTP] assists our B-2 pilots [to] remain ready for B-2 combat missions. It provides B-2 pilots with flying hour experience and decision-making in dynamic environments. The small fleet of B-2s provides a limited number of flights per pilot, per month. The T-38 helps to augment flying hours and the perishable nature of the skill sets pilots can only get while flying in a challenging, dynamic environment. T-38 training flights give pilots additional opportunities to refine their skills in airmanship, flight leadership, cockpit resource management, and basic hand flying, stick and rudder.

"When a new pilot arrives at Whiteman to fly the B-2, they are first enrolled in T-38 Initial Qualification Training. A cadre of instructor pilots assigned to the 13th Bomb Squadron train each new pilot until they have reached the required proficiency. Once pilots have gained more experience in the T-38 they are enrolled in additional upgrade programmes, including two-ship formation, four-ship formation, and low-level. These upgrades challenge pilots and further refine their aviation and decision-making skills."

The resident 13th Bomb Squadron has a training element known as Detachment 12 which runs the IQT programme. Over a six-month course pilots complete 266 hours of academics, sit 30 exams, undertake 46 simulator missions and 10 flights in the aircraft.

After completion of their IQT, pilots are assigned to either the 110th or 393rd Bomb Squadron where they embark on a mission qualification training programme. In their monthly flying duty, a B-2 pilot evenly splits simulator time and flight-time. In a typical month pilots receive two or three flights in both the aircraft and the simulator. The B-2 simulator provides pilots with a high-fidelity, dynamic training environment.

One of three B-2 bombers deployed from Whiteman Air Force Base, Missouri, is prepped for a training mission at Joint Base Pearl Harbor-Hickam, Hawaii. US Air Force/Senior Airman Thomas Barley

assigned to the 419th Flight Test Squadron, based at Edwards Air Force Base, California. It was no ordinary re-assignment; *Spirit of Pennsylvania* is the first B-2 to cycle through three programmed depot maintenance overhauls, which included restoration of its airframe, electrical and mechanical systems inspections, and restoration of the aircraft's low observable system, including removal and reapplication of the radar absorbing materials.

The US Air Force is well aware of the threat posed by evolving threat technologies to the B-2's second-generation stealth capability, reducing its ability to penetrate anti-access/area denial (A2/AD) environments. Such realisation led to the 2019 decision to replace the B-2 with the B-21 Raider in the 2030s, even though the Spirit will be capable of operating into the late 2050s. Originally designed for a

20,000 flight-hour service life, each B-2 has been extended to some 40,000 hours.

UPGRADES

To ensure the fleet can accomplish its nuclear and conventional mission in highly defended and anti-access environments, periodic modernisation efforts must be undertaken to upgrade combat capability as well as improve the viability, supportability, and survivability of the weapon system.

Director Operational Test and Evaluation approved the B-2 Defensive Management System-Modernisation (DMS-M) Milestone B Test and Evaluation Master Plan in October 2015, followed by approval from the Under Secretary of Defense for Acquisition, Technology, and Logistics for the engineering, manufacturing, and development phase on March 24, 2016.

"The long-range B-2 has an unrefuelled range of 5,200nm but with a single aerial refuelling, the Spirit can fly 8,600nm."

Spirit of Texas taxies to the runway at Joint Base Pearl Harbor-Hickam, Hawaii for a Bomber Task Force mission. US Air Force/Lieutenant Allen Palmer

DMS-M funding began in FY2008, and the systems were scheduled to be fielded in FY2022. Official US government documentation stated the modernisation was a principal enabler of survivability for the B-2 aircraft.

DMS-M upgrades were to include a digital electronic support measures (ESM) subsystem, new ESM antennas, and modern display processing units to improve threat radar detection, identification, and avoidance capabilities.

Associated software components were designed to integrate the upgraded systems with existing B-2 avionics systems to improve overall pilot threat awareness, threat reaction, and survivability. Northrop Grumman was the prime contractor and integrator. DMS-M programme underwent a re-baseline in FY2017 caused by delays and cost overruns such that the FY2021 budget terminated the DMS-M programme with funding realigned to address reliability and sustainment of the B-2 cockpit display system until end-of-life. Only *Spirit of Pennsylvania* received a prototype DMS-M upgrade.

Air Force Global Strike Command, owner of the B-2 fleet said the omission of DMS-M does not detract from the aircraft's survivability in the future because the US Air Force funded other systems to increase the aircraft's survivability against emerging threats.

These included an advanced processor to provide the necessary power to increase situational awareness on eight new primary crew station flight displays under the B-2 Display Modernization (BDM) programme, and low-observable signature modifications.

According to the Department of Defense FY2024 USAF budget estimate: "The current displays, known as multi-function display units [MDUs] are experiencing significant obsolescence issues that are unsustainable. Increasing failure rates and reliance on the legacy cathode ray tube technology with no industry base has led to increased

Crew chiefs assigned to the 509th Aircraft Maintenance Squadron prepare Spirit of Georgia at Whiteman Air Force Base, Missouri. US Air Force/SSgt Sadie Colbert

cannibalization actions and degraded aircraft readiness status.

"Under the current plan, the BDM will undergo combined developmental and initial operational test and evaluation in 1QFY2025, followed by operational test and evaluation in 2QFY2025."

Lockheed Martin is supplying advanced graphics processors and modernised displays to provide adequate computer power to give the crew a much greater level of situational awareness and reduced vulnerability in dense threat environments. Information displayed is fed from the aircraft's mission transfer and beyond line-of-sight mission planning systems.

The FY2024 USAF budget estimate states: "The Low Observable Signature and Supportability Modifications [LOSSM] program supports the B-2's ability to penetrate anti-access combat environments, performing missions directed by the National Command Authority while ensuring aircrew survivability. The LOSSM program reduces low observable [LO] maintenance man hours, increases aircraft availability, and maintains and improves the combat-ready LO signature for the B-2 fleet."

The LOSSM programme includes multiple improvements that include:

• Improved LO materials (conductive gap fillers and tape, adhesives, electrically resistive materials, radar absorbing material, fastener fills, coatings, and improved processes).

• LO structures (radar radomes, hot trailing edges and tiles, intermediate section doors, tailpipes, windows, bay panels, permanent fasteners, exhaust pockets, gust load alleviation system, inlets, radar absorbing structures, antenna optimisation, overall signature stability, and alternate high frequency material expansion).

• Radio frequency (RF) diagnostic tools, a near-field radar evaluation system, a flight line tier one material inspection system, a signature diagnostic system, a portable Laser removal tool, next generation Tier II and Tier III systems, a handheld imaging tool, and LO-related special test equipment.

LOSSM installations will take place at Air Force Plant 42, the B-2 depot in Palmdale, California, and Whiteman Air Force Base. The US Air Force says LOSSM is the most substantial signature improvement of the B-2 in its 30-year history.

An F-15C Eagle assigned to the then 493rd Fighter Squadron, flies alongside a B-2 Spirit during a Bomber Task Force mission over the North Sea in August 2021. US Air Force/SSgt Rachel Maxwell

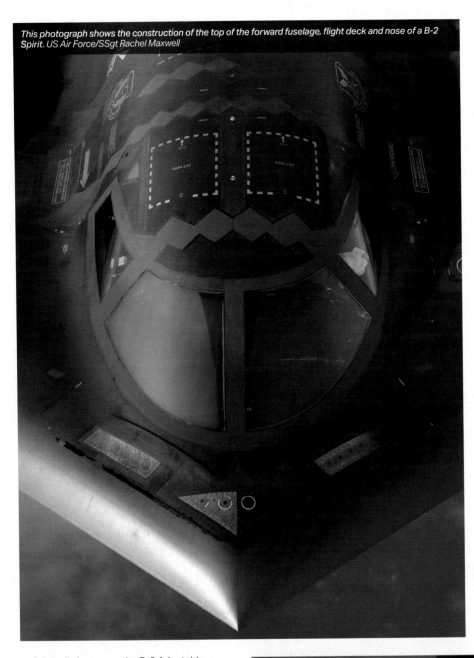

This photograph shows the construction of the top of the forward fuselage, flight deck and nose of a B-2 Spirit. US Air Force/SSgt Rachel Maxwell

requirements. B2C3 is designed to deliver the open mission systems (OMS) architecture (domain) within the B-2.

Sierra Nevada Corporation is the prime contractor for ACS 4.0 and is set to receive an engineering and manufacturing development (EMD) contract in 3QFY2023.

Development of the AITG is planned to begin in Q1FY2024.

Installation of the B2C3 is required on all B-2 aircraft but current funding covers ten aircraft (two EMD and eight production). Spiral 1 development began in October 2022 and the production/fielding phase is planned for Q1FY2024.

OPERATIONS

Northrop Grumman's B-2 first entered combat during Operation Allied Force – the Kosovo conflict – on March 24, 1999 and demonstrated its capability for accurately delivering bombs on high-value targets. That said, during a mission flown on May 7-8, 1999, five JDAMs struck the Chinese embassy in Belgrade in error.

After flying combat operations against targets in Afghanistan, Iraq, and Libya, B-2s flew no combat missions between April 2011 and early 2017.

This changed on January 17–18, 2017 when two B-2s launched from Whiteman Air Force Base on a round-robin mission to strike a terrorist camp in Libya, under Operation Odyssey Dawn.

A third B-2 also launched from Whiteman as an air spare, before turning for home. Two ground spare aircraft were held on readiness as back-ups.

The two strikers, radio call signs Clip 11 and Clip 12 flew through international airspace until turning to hit their target near Sirte on Libya's central coast. The two B-2s struck their allocated target through a light cloud cover at midnight local time. A total of 85 GBU-38 500lb JDAMs were released and impacted the target in under a minute. No other aircraft could have delivered so many guided munitions simultaneously on a single pass over a target while retaining the element of surprise.

Given the conflict in Libya involved outside powers with access to early warning sensors

Originally known as the B-2 Adaptable Communications Suite, today the programme is named B-2 Advanced Communications and is designed to support and enhance the aircraft's communications capabilities. According to the FY2024 USAF budget estimate, programme requirements include secure beyond-line-of-sight (BLOS) and line-of-sight (LOS) communications, and the ability to communicate and operate in the Joint All-Domain Command and Control (JADC2) environment throughout all mission phases.

There are three primary modernisation efforts underway: the Adaptable Communications Suite 4.0 (ACS) intended to retain secure BLOS communication capabilities via the multiple user objective system (MUOS) satellite constellation; the Airborne Integrated Terminal Group (AITG) replacement. The current AITG provides LOS UHF communications and very high frequency (VHF) anti-jam, encrypted, and unencrypted voice communications; and the B-2 Collaborative Combat Communication (B2C3) system which seeks to identify, leverage, and integrate existing capabilities (such as ACS 4.0 and AITG) to meet B-2 communications

The refuelling probe of a KC-135 Stratotanker plugged into the air refuelling receptacle of a B-2 Spirit during an aerial refuelling flight. The B-2 multi-role bomber can deliver both conventional and nuclear munitions. US Air Force/Lieutenant Sam Eckholm

GLOBAL POWER MISSIONS

B-2s fly long-range missions, an essential requirement to Air Force Global Strike Command's Global Power Mission set. Extensive effort and debate have been devoted to determining what the safe crew endurance limit should be.

During mission qualification training B-2 pilots undertake a 24-hour long endurance simulator mission which is designed to train pilots with the characteristics of a combat mission. These include multiple aerial refuellings, managing updates to the mission, long-range communications, target area employment, entry and exit runs for common target sets, and landing.

Working at the instructor console, an instructor pilot will input emergencies to evaluate the pilots' ability to keep the aircraft mission capable. Evaluators determine the pilots' ability to overcome the emergency, and safely continue with the tasking. The emergency is introduced by the mission's 20-hour point to enable evaluators to determine the pilots' diagnosis and decision-making processes.

A 509th BW spokesperson told Janes: "The long endurance simulator mission is often the pilot's first time managing physical and mental fatigue while flying."

During the 24-hour simulation, tests are performed on the pilots to determine how their body might react to being airborne for 24 hours. Tests are completed to determine the effect of diet, sleep cycles, and sleep deprivation on each pilot's ability to perform the mission.

The spokesperson continued: "The US Air Force Flight Operations manual 11-203 V3 provides guidance on the flight duty period [the maximum duration allowed: normal/augmented] and crew rest requirements. Crews typically undertake mission planning leading up to a long duration mission and are required a minimum 12-hour crew rest prior to the flight duty period. If the flight is occurring in a time that does not sync with the normal sleep/wake cycle, crews are typically given a few nights to help shift their circadian rhythm."

Global power missions require a meticulous mission plan created by a mission planning cell (MPC) - a group of airmen assigned to the 509th Operational Support Squadron. The MPC's main tasks are to plan the route to get the aircraft to the target area, source imagery of the target area, analyse the target and create a threat assessment.

Mission planning can take up to 72 hours to complete.

After a succession of briefings, the pilots leave the combined operations build about an hour before the take-off time and are driven directly to the jets. On arrival at their aircraft the mission crew do not start the engines and get the aircraft's systems running, other crews complete these tasks. A crew typically taxi the aircraft about 20 minutes before take-off time.

Dubbed the deadliest building on earth because it combines the manpower and the firepower of the Spirit Force, the B-2 Combined Operations Building was opened at Whiteman on April 23, 2021. The 8,000sq ft facility houses flight records, aircraft trainers, combat plans, weather forecasting, airfield management, the step desk, long range communications, intelligence, mission planning, aircrew flight equipment, admin offices and aircrew alert facilities.

The building is installed with 483 miles of fibre optic line used to transfer massive amounts of data between the various units that include intelligence, operations, and the aircrew at high-speed: a primary requirement for communication and mission planning.

and secure communications, even a little warning could have undercut the effectiveness of the strike.

As the B-2s pulled off the target, they were followed by several General Atomics MQ-9 Reaper unmanned combat air vehicles (UCAVs) used to destroy any vehicles escaping the bomb attack, and to provide battle damage assessment using their on-board sensors. The B-2s returned to Whiteman at the end of a 33-hour round-trip during which the aircraft refuelled five times.

General Tod Wolters ret'd, the then supreme allied commander in Europe, said: "The precision strike demonstrated that the US Air Force can put any target at risk, plus or minus a second, plus or minus a millimetre."

Unstated, the mission also showed potential threats worldwide what global delivery of precision firepower actually means.

Until the April 2020 announcement that the United States was scaling back its continuous bomber presence in the western Pacific, B-2s had been deploying to Guam – where typhoon-proof hangars were built for them in 2005. Deployments continued with the objective of being operationally

> ## "No other aircraft could have delivered so many guided munitions simultaneously on a single pass over a target while retaining the element of surprise."

unpredictable, demonstrated by two B-2s deploying to Europe on May 7, 2020. Other B-2 deployments in 2020 included one to Diego Garcia, an island in the British Indian Ocean Territory, which had been used for previous missions in the US Central Command area of responsibility.

While the US Air Force has said nothing about changing B-2 tactics to accompany its change in deployment schedule, it is possible that the final decade of its service may see a greater emphasis on its low-level penetration capabilities. An aspect of the stealth bomber built into the design back in the 1980s, when it was envisioned that a force of 192 B-2s could

hold at risk any number of Soviet relocatable intercontinental ballistic missile launchers.

RED FLAG
Red Flag is a large-scale exercise that offers participants an opportunity to enhance their integrated mission planning capabilities with the use of ever-evolving intelligence. In February 2022, the 393rd Bomb Squadron participated in Exercise Red Flag 2022-1 at Nellis Air Force Base, Nevada. This remains the most recent iteration of Red Flag attended by the 509th BW following the mishap involving *Spirit of New York* at Whiteman Air Force Base on December 10, 2022, after which the fleet was grounded.

Maintainers perform post-flight procedures on a B-2 at Whiteman Air Force Base, Missouri.
US Air National Guard/Airman 1st Class Kelly Ferguson

Airmen assigned to the 437th Airlift Wing stationed at Joint Base Charleston, South Carolina, and 509th Bomb Wing, stationed at Whiteman Air Force Base, Missouri, conduct a specialised fuel operation from a C-17A Globemaster III to a B-2 Spirit at Edwards Air Force Base, California. This was the first time a C-17 had refuelled a B-2, a capability that increases the flexibility for the bomber to conduct agile combat employment operations. US Air Force/Airman 1st Class Mitchell Corley

A B-2 taxies past the dock for Spirit of Texas at Whiteman Air Force Base. US Air National Guard/MSgt John Hillier

Discussing the squadron's participation, Lieutenant Colonel Christopher Conant, 393rd Expeditionary Bomb Squadron commander said: "In the B-2 community, we say, 'mission planning is our primary tactic' and our quality of mission planning is what sets us apart. Preparing our mission with the best plan possible, with the best data possible, is important because that can reduce challenges and errors, as variables on the battlefield inevitably change. Our mission planning philosophy combines the tenants of

flexibility with a holistic perspective on how to execute a joint air campaign.

"Intelligence plays a critical role early in the mission planning process. Initial assessments are what we base facts and assumptions on, to then build the plan. But intel never stops. As the mission planning progresses, we are constantly updating and refining our products so we can adjust.

"Red Flag trains our air crew and intelligence officers to mission plan with

their counterparts from fellow air force units, which tests their integration capabilities on a grander platform within a stable environment. For the 393rd, it is important to learn from other air crews and understand how their aircraft can assist and benefit the execution of the B-2 mission."

Explaining how intel and operations go hand in hand, Major Jonathan Waag, 509th Operation Support Squadron chief of intelligence said: "Red Flag provides us the opportunity to practice our processes as unit level intel and develop our analytical skills at the tactical level. The mission planning process at Red Flag allows us to network among the intel community and learn from our collective experiences."

According to Lieutenant Colonel Conant, the wing prioritises multi-aircraft integrations because they offer the most realistic and valuable training for the airmen. The B-2 primarily integrates with other low observable platforms, the F-35 and F-22. These integrations are typically conducted four to five times a year, one of the biggest being Red Flag. As airframes modernise, so have the mission planning tactics to optimise the new stealth capabilities. Much like tactics and aircraft capabilities, the technology used by intelligence analysts has also improved with new variants of remotely piloted aircraft, satellites and communication networks providing more

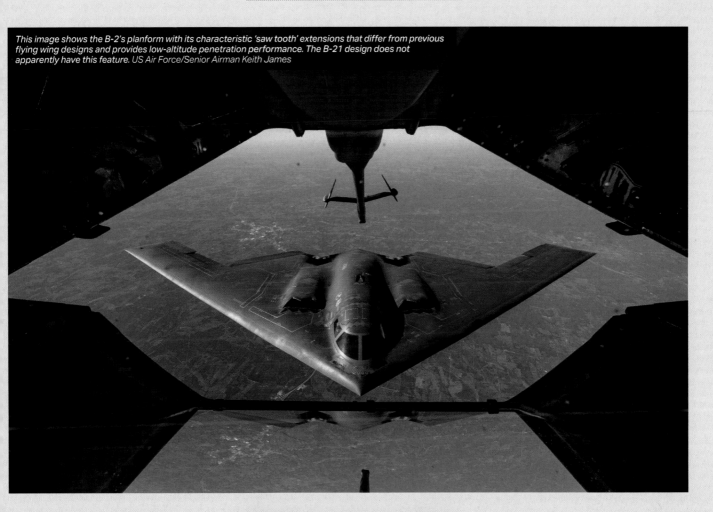

This image shows the B-2's planform with its characteristic 'saw tooth' extensions that differ from previous flying wing designs and provides low-altitude penetration performance. The B-21 design does not apparently have this feature. US Air Force/Senior Airman Keith James

timely and accurate information before, during and after mission flights.

50-HOUR MISSION
A B-2 Spirit flew from Whiteman Air Force Base, Missouri, to Royal Australian Air Force Base Amberley, Australia on March 23, 2022, to execute training with the Royal Australian Air Force (RAAF) to increase interoperability and to operate forward in the Indo-Pacific region. Once inside Australian airspace, the B-2 rendezvoused with a KC-135 Stratotanker from the Alaska Air National Guard's 168th Air Refuelling Wing to complete aerial refuelling before integrating with eight fighter aircraft — two RAAF F-35A Lightning IIs, two EA-18 Growlers, two F/A-18F Super Hornets and two US Air Force F-16C aggressors —to conduct training operations.

After the integration, the B-2 then landed at RAAF Base Amberley: a first-time event. A crew swap was performed with the new

> *"Barksdale Air Force Base is also home to a new facility designed and constructed to support the B-2 Spirit."*

crew flying the aircraft back to Whiteman. During the return leg, the B-2 integrated with F-22 Raptors from Joint Base Pearl Harbor-Hickam, Hawaii.

This mission was a demonstration of the US Air Force's global reach capability and the ability to address complex and uncertain security environments.

JOINT INTEGRATION EXERCISE
On April 4, the 509th Bomb Wing began a four-day interoperability exercise involving active duty, Air National Guard and Air Force Reserve fighter, bomber, air refuelling and support units from across the United States.

The exercise was designed to enable high-fidelity distributed mission planning, coordinated long-range standoff munitions integration, dynamic targeting and advanced survival, evasion, resistance, and escape scenarios. The event also provided for the development of new and non-traditional communications tactics, techniques, and procedures.

The resident B-2 Spirit, A-10 Thunderbolt II aircraft, and US Army UH-60 Black Hawk helicopters were joined by six F-35A Lightning II aircraft assigned to the 388th

A B-2 lands at Whiteman Air Force Base following a round trip to Libya during Operation Odyssey Dawn. US Air Force/Senior Airman Joel Pfiester

Airmen from the active duty 509th and Air National Guard 131st Bomb Wings operate a jet fuel pump on the flight line at RAF Fairford, England during a Bomber Task Force Europe deployment in March 2020. US Air Force/SSgt Kayla White

> "The B-2 Combined Operations Building is dubbed the deadliest building on earth because it combines the manpower and the firepower of the Spirit Force."

Fighter Wing based at Hill Air Force Base, Utah, two T-38 Talon's from Langley Air Force Base, Virginia and one KC-10 Extender assigned to the 60th Air Mobility Wing based at Travis Air Force Base, California. The combined fleets worked out of Whiteman for the duration of the exercise. Other flying units were staged out of McConnell, Dyess, Ellsworth, and Barksdale.

Commenting on the Agile Tiger exercise, Colonel Daniel Diehl, 509th Bomb Wing Commander said: "As America's premier

bomb wing, our airmen are trusted to execute nuclear and conventional airpower, and we are constantly looking for ways to improve processes and ensure we're meeting the objectives of the National Defence Strategy. Exercise Agile Tiger was designed to ensure we stay combat ready, every day.

"By bringing the different players here, we can see where the gaps and seams in our training are, how our airmen need to innovate in order to win in the future and take those lessons and start applying them."

The exercise assessed operational unpredictability through the application of agile combat employment concepts. When this application is done to training, it creates an adaptable, prepared joint force to credibly deter adversaries.

Explaining, Major General Andrew Gerbera, 8th Air Force and Joint-Global Strike Operations Center commander said: "Our agile combat employment efforts provide on-call combat operations around the globe. Agile, back-to-basics training gets us to where

This photograph shows the B-2's air intake layout, which from a design perspective had to reconcile stealth with the need to provide sufficient air for four engines. Similar compromises had to be made with the aircraft's exhaust design, which is why images of them are not published. US Air Force/Senior Airman Joel Pfiester

we need to be. This exercise proves we can seamlessly integrate with other weapons systems in the field when called upon."

A key objective of Agile Tiger is to replicate and predict real-world scenarios from mission conception to execution.

Operators and intelligence airmen designed complex scenarios to mimic contested combat environments, both in the air and on the ground. The A-10Cs, Black Hawks and Joint Terminal Attack Controller units engaged in advanced survival, evasion, resistance, and escape

scenarios. Pilots collaborated through high-fidelity mission planning, crafting their best attack plan. Once in the air, B-2 Spirits and F-35A Lightning IIs integrated with B-1B Lancers and B-52H Stratofortress's for coordinated attacks including long-range stand-off munitions.

Throughout the exercise, on-going communication and operability was critical. An E-3 Sentry provided a real-time threat picture and coordination of the battlespace.

Colonel Diehl said: "It's important for me as the wing commander to ensure that the B-2

maintains its competitive advantage for years to come. We are still the leading edge of the fight, as it needs to be. We are still making sure that we are the force that can fight tonight, and the more opportunity we provide to have realistic training scenarios ensures we can maintain that competitive advantage.".

SPIRIT REALM

Barksdale Air Force Base, home of Air Force Global Strike Command (AFGSC) and the B-52H-equipped 2nd Bomb Wing

Airmen operate a fuel pump while refuelling B-2 Spirit 88-0332/WM Spirit of Washington at RAF Fairford, England during a Bomber Task Force Europe deployment in March 2020. US Air Force/SSgt Kayla White

SPIRIT FIREPOWER

Designed and built by Northrop Grumman, the B-2 is a two-pilot, long-range, all-weather bomber designed to employ both conventional and nuclear precision-guided weapons. It incorporates stealth technologies to reduce radar cross section and minimise electronic, infrared, acoustic, and visual signatures.

B-2 mission systems include a GPS-aided precision navigation system, strategic radar targeting system, electronic support measures, and worldwide communications and data transfer systems.

The B-2 is the only long-range strike aircraft capable of penetrating and surviving today's advanced integrated air defence systems to deliver weapons against heavily defended targets, many of which are hardened or deeply buried. It is also the only bomber able to carry two 30,000lb Boeing GBU-57A/B Massive Ordnance Penetrator (MOP) weapons, the largest conventional bomb known to be in existence.

Its general weapons payload is up to 40,000lb carried in internal bomb bays. Conventional weapon payloads include 80 500lb GBU-38 JDAMs carried on four smart bomb rack assemblies, 16 2,000lb GBU-31 JDAMs mounted on two rotary launcher assemblies.

As part of the Flexible Strike Phase 1 upgrade, B-2s were modified to carry up to 192 Small Diameter Bombs, either Boeing GBU-39s or Raytheon GBU-53s, and up to 16 Lockheed Martin AGM-158 (JASSM-ER) missiles. Eventually, the Spirit will be able to carry GBU-56 Laser JDAMs, and JDAM-5000s fitted with Hard Target Void Sensing Fuses.

Each bomb bay houses a single rotary launcher assembly which can carry eight precision-guided weapons like the AGM-154 Joint Stand-Off Weapon or the AGM-158 Joint Air-to-Surface Standoff Missile. Alternately a bomb bay can house two smart bomb rack assemblies, one forward, one aft, each able to carry 20 GBU-38 JDAMs.

At the point of weapon release, each type of assembly functions differently. A rotary launcher assembly uses an explosive charge to drive two pistons that drive the bombs out of the bay. A smart bomb rack assembly uses an electrical release mechanism.

Currently, the B-2 is the only bomber capable of delivering nuclear gravity bombs, the megaton-class B83-1 and up to eight B-61-7s or earth-penetrating B61-11s. The Flexible Strike Phase 1 upgrade enabled the aircraft to carry the improved B61-12, designed to defeat multiple target types, including those buried deep underground.

Source: US Air Force

B-2 Spirit 82-1070/WM *Spirit of Ohio takes off from RAF Fairford, England, on March 13, 2020 during a Bomber Task Force Europe deployment.* US Air National Guard/TSgt Colton Elliott

"Currently, the B-2 is the only bomber capable of delivering nuclear gravity bombs, the megaton-class B83-1 and up to eight B-61-7s or earth-penetrating B61-11s."

B-2 SPIRIT FLEET

Serial number	Air vehicle number	Name	Events
82-1066	AV-1	*Spirit of America*	
82-1067	AV-2	*Spirit of Arizona*	
82-1068	AV-3	*Spirit of New York*	Damaged on December 10, 2022, after the crew was forced to make an emergency landing at Whiteman Air Force Base, Missouri following an in-flight malfunction during routine operations.
82-1069	AV-4	*Spirit of Indiana*	
82-1070	AV-5	*Spirit of Ohio*	
82-1071	AV-6	*Spirit of Mississippi*	
88-0328	AV-7	*Spirit of Texas*	
88-0329	AV-8	*Spirit of Missouri*	
88-0330	AV-9	*Spirit of California*	
88-0331	AV-10	*Spirit of South Carolina*	
88-0332	AV-11	*Spirit of Washington*	
89-0127	AV-12	*Spirit of Kansas*	Crashed on take-off at Andersen Air Base, Guam on February 23, 2008
89-0128	AV-13	*Spirit of Nebraska*	
89-0129	AV-14	*Spirit of Georgia*	Landing gear collapsed at Whiteman in September 2021 which damaged the wing. Undergoing repair at Palmdale Plant 42
90-0040	AV-15	*Spirit of Alaska*	
90-0041	AV-16	*Spirit of Hawaii*	Completed an emergency landing at Whiteman Air Force Base in December 2022 and suffered damage to the wing.
92-0700	AV-17	*Spirit of Florida*	
93-1085	AV-18	*Spirit of Oklahoma*	
93-1086	AV-19	*Spirit of Kitty Hawk*	
93-1087	AV-20	*Spirit of Pennsylvania*	
93-1088	AV-21	*Spirit of Louisiana*	

Notes
Comprising just 20 aircraft, the B-2 fleet is small. Nineteen aircraft are assigned to the active duty 509th Bomb Wing (BW) and the Missouri Air National Guard's 131st BW. The two wings operate as a Total Force Association, the 509th BW is the sponsor organisation and the 131st BW is the associate organisation. One aircraft is permanently assigned to the 419th Flight Test Squadron based at Edwards Air Force Base, California. The available fleet is short of that number because some aircraft are in depot level maintenance at Palmdale Plant 42.

is also home to a new facility designed and constructed to support the B-2 Spirit. First announced on December 3, 2022, this software factory known as Spirit Realm, was built by the B-2 Weapons Systems Support Center (WSSC), a division of the Air Force Life Cycle Management Center (AFLCM) based at Wright-Patterson Air Force Base, Ohio, and the B-2 manufacturer, Northrop Grumman.

The WSSC designed Spirit Realm to meet three primary objectives: to reduce the flight test risks and timelines; to minimise the burden on the B-2 flight test team based at Edwards Air Force Base, California; and to increase the quality of integrated functional capability by conducting high-frequency automated testing. The objectives seek to enable decisive capability upgrades to the B-2 Spirit.

In accordance with the DoD's software modernisation strategy released on February 2, 2022, Spirit Realm uses a software engineering practice that aims to unify software development (Dev), security (Sec) and operations (Ops) dubbed DevSecOps which is referred to by the Department of Defense as its reference design.

According to the DoD chief information officer: "The main characteristic of DevSecOps is to automate, monitor, and apply security at all phases of the software lifecycle: plan, develop, build, test, release, deliver, deploy, operate, and monitor."

In an Air Force Global Strike Command press release Captain Joel Graley, the lead of a B-2 software maintenance and innovation team with the B-2 programme office at AFLCMC said: "B-2 software is now developed, tested, and integrated using modern scaled agile principles and a single software baseline. This approach enables the fielding of the highest priority capabilities at an unprecedented pace and ensures the B-2 can rapidly field new capabilities to counter emerging threats."

According to AFGSC, the new software factory has cut software upgrade timelines from two years to three months, averted more than $18m in annual flight test costs, and yielded more tests with fewer defects, resulting in better overall operational capability for the B-2 fleet.

B-2 Spirit 82-1070/WM Spirit of Ohio at RAF Fairford, England, on March 13, 2020 during a Bomber Task Force Europe deployment. US Air National Guard/TSgt Colton Elliott

Crew chiefs assigned to the 509th and 131st Aircraft Maintenance Squadrons recover a B-2 at RAF Fairford, England. US Air National Guard/TSgt Colton Elliott

The B-21 Raider was unveiled to the public at a ceremony on December 2, 2022, in Palmdale, California. Designed to operate in tomorrow's high-end threat environment, the B-21 will play a critical role in ensuring America's enduring air power capability. US Air Force

NEW-GEN STEALTH BOMBER

David Isby and Mark Ayton detail America's nascent B-21 Raider stealth bomber and its public debut.

what it means to be able to bring this kind of capability very quickly and be able to adapt it vis-à-vis the threat. It'll be the backbone of our bomber fleet."

The world and its threats have changed dramatically since the last new bomber, the B-2 Spirit, was introduced in 1988, as has the way the US Air Force, other US military services and allies work together as a joint, multi-domain force. Senior defence officials say that new thinking and innovation are needed to meet the new and emerging threats.

The B-21 is the first new bomber to be introduced to service since the end of the Cold War. US Air Force officials envision an ultimate fleet of at least 100 aircraft with an average procurement unit cost requirement of $692m (base year 2022 dollars).

DESIGN

The B-21 is designed to be a more capable and adaptable, state-of-the-art aircraft that will gradually replace the aging B-1B Lancer and B-2 Spirit bombers in service.

According to design requirements, the B-21 is a long-range, highly survivable stealth bomber capable of delivering a mix of conventional and nuclear munitions. The aircraft will play a major role supporting national security objectives and assuring US allies and partners across the globe.

According to the Secretary of the Air Force media affairs: "The aircraft has updated stealth qualities and mission flexibility that senior leaders in the US Air Force and across the Department of Defense say are necessary to achieve the US goal of achieving integrated deterrence, and if necessary, capabilities required to successfully respond to aggression anywhere in the world at any time.

"The aircraft unveiled on December 2 is one of six under production. Each is considered a test aircraft, but each is being built on the same production line, using the same tools, processes, and technicians who will build production standard aircraft. This approach has enabled production engineers and technicians to capture lessons learned and apply them directly to follow-on aircraft, driving home a focus on repeatability, producibility and quality.

"Timing of the first flight will be data and event driven, not date driven.

While the precise date when the B-21 will enter service is unknown, basing decisions have been made. On March 27, 2019, the secretary of the air force announced that Ellsworth Air Force Base, South Dakota, Whiteman, Missouri and Dyess Texas are the preferred main operating base locations.

Ellsworth was approved as MOB 1 on June 3, 2021, and become the formal training unit for the B-21. Each will receive aircraft as they become available.

In addition to building a bomber with state-of-the-art technology and capabilities, US Air Force officials have emphasised the focus on containing costs while simultaneously allowing for maximum flexibility.

As an example, the B-21 is designed with an open systems architecture that will enable rapid future capability integration to keep pace with the highly contested threat environment.

The B-21's design is based on firm requirements with existing and mature technology to control programme costs. Northrop Grumman has been directed to use production processes, production tooling, and a production workforce that ensures sustained production while avoiding unnecessary costs.

n a display of America's resolve in meeting security threats, on December 2, 2022, the US Air Force publicly unveiled the B-21 Raider. The aircraft represents the first new, long-range strike bomber in a generation and is specifically designed to be the multifunctional backbone of the modernised bomber fleet.

While the B-21 is not expected to be operational and introduced into service for several more years, the formal unveiling ceremony hosted by Northrop Grumman at its Palmdale, California facility was a significant milestone in the US Air Force's effort to modernise combat capabilities.

During the ceremony, Secretary of Defense, Lloyd Austin said: "The B-21 Raider is the first strategic bomber in more than three decades. It is a testament to America's enduring advantages in ingenuity and innovation and is proof of the department's long-term commitment to building advanced capabilities that will fortify America's ability to deter aggression, today and into the future."

Before the event, US Air Force Chief of Staff General CQ Brown said: "When I think about accelerate change, this is exactly

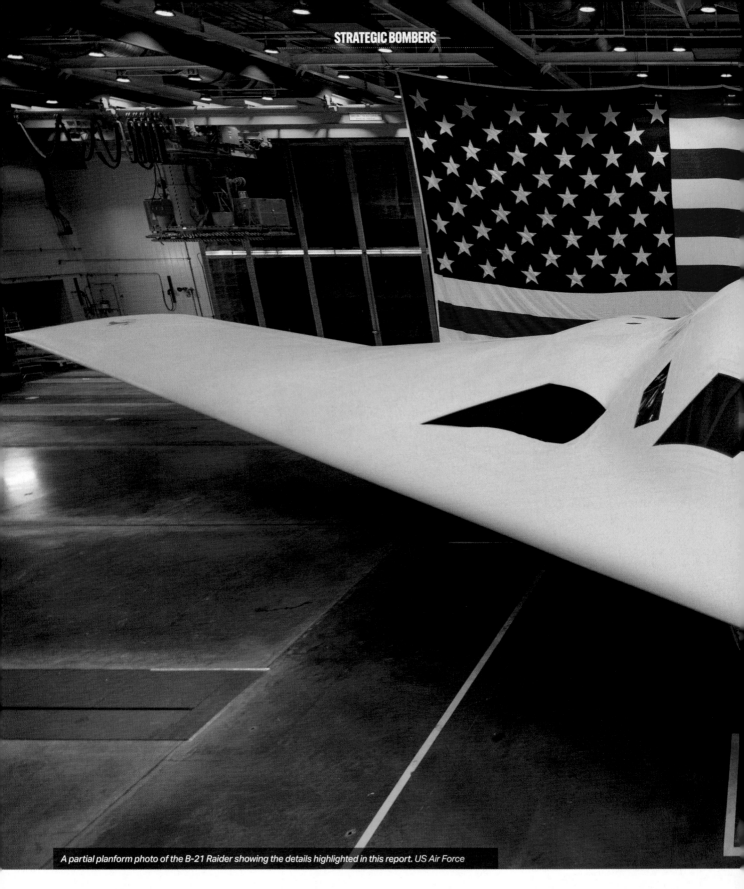

A partial planform photo of the B-21 Raider showing the details highlighted in this report. US Air Force

Assistant Secretary of the Air Force for Acquisition, Technology and Logistic Andrew Hunter said: "Leveraging innovative manufacturing techniques, open systems architectures and active management allows us to integrate new technology as it matures and ensures the B-21 can adapt to future threats and be successful when and where we need it."

PRODUCTION, BASES, AND MISSION

During an August 13, 2020, video conference, Randy Walden, head of the US Air Force Rapid Capabilities Office (RCO) said: "It's starting to look like an aeroplane."

Walden is one of the few people briefed on what is happening inside the secure Plant 42 at Northrop Grumman's Palmdale, California site. Walden's office is responsible for managing the highly-classified special access programme. Part of what's referred to as the black world of activities not openly discussed or, often, even revealed.

While no timeline has been announced, the 420th Flight Test Squadron was reactivated at Edwards Air Force Base, California on October 4, 2019, and has been designated as the B-21 Combined Test Force. The 420th will operate from a remote area of the base in both new and renovated buildings and is busy preparing to lead the testing.

The B-21's systems have already been ground tested and flight testing has apparently already begun on a modified surrogate testbed aircraft, reportedly a civil-registered Boeing 737.

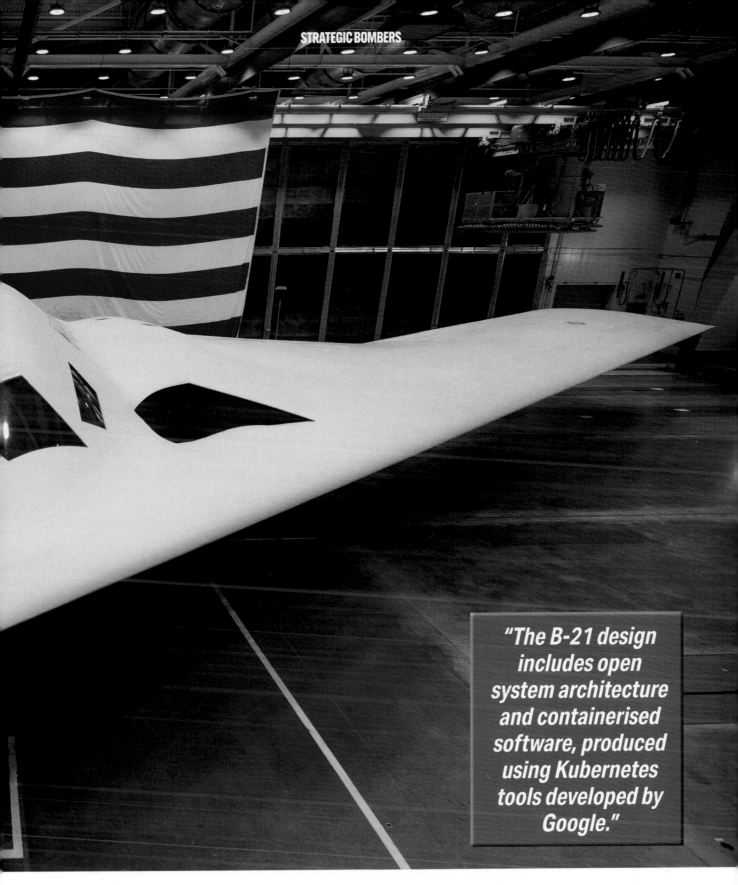

"The B-21 design includes open system architecture and containerised software, produced using Kubernetes tools developed by Google."

A non-flying prototype has also been built at Plant 42 to correct full-scale system integration issues.

The B-21 design includes open system architecture and containerised software, produced using Kubernetes tools developed by Google. Kubernetes is an open-source system for automating deployment, scaling, and management of containerised applications. Containerised software allows upgrades to be integrated but without affecting the millions of lines of software code required to make the B-21 function.

If no setbacks are encountered and following-on from the six aircraft already on the Palmdale assembly line, B-21 low-rate initial production (LRIP) could start during FY2023-2024, with initial operational capability (IOC) following within three years.

Its production rate could ramp up to 12-14 aircraft per year once the bomber enters full rate production (FRP). The programme of record remains for 100 aircraft, though multiple studies have identified that an expanded bomber force is needed to meet changing US defence planning and priorities, especially for east Asia and the Pacific Rim.

"Programmes will always have a few surprises early on, and the B-21 won't be any different. I know we're not going to be immune from design flaws," Walden said, "we're going to have to work through those."

The B-21 programme schedule – and the big-ticket requirement that production aircraft meet a flyaway cost of no more than $550m (in FY2010 dollars) – is challenging. Some of the B-21 subcontractors, Walden said, had experienced delays imposed by the COVID-19 pandemic.

Wichita-based Spirit Aero Systems used Defense Production Act funding to repurpose some of its facility for the B-21. Before the pandemic, the facility was used to produce composite structures for the Boeing 737 MAX.

"So far, we think the programme is on track, coming in under or at the unit cost we thought it would come in at, which is great. We think it's going to deliver the capabilities because we have a strong set of requirements that underpin it," said General Mark Weatherington, then commander of Air Force Global Strike Command.

Reportedly only the air force chief of staff is authorised to change B-21 requirements to prevent a 'requirements creep' caused by moving goalposts and requiring expensive and time-consuming changes, the poisoned chalice for many Department of Defense programmes.

> ## "The B-21 Raider is the first strategic bomber in more than three decades."

WHAT'S COMING?

The day when a B-21's wheels are on a flight line is getting closer, but the landing gear and the aircraft they are going to be attached to can only be seen in the images released by the US Air Force which we have used to illustrate this feature.

B-21 photos released by the US Air Force show a smaller, modified version of the B-2 stealth bomber, indicating it is intended to conduct similar missions, flying at high-altitude for precision weapons delivery.

In 2019, head of Northrop Grumman's aerospace sector, Janis Pamiljans was quoted in the press as saying: "What we learned on B-2 are baselined in the design of the B-21 for the purposes of supportability, sustainability, and mission capable rate. Where the B-2 goes, so goes B-21."

Further analysis of the illustrations released show each main landing gear unit has two wheels, rather than four as per the B-2 which suggests a lower max take-off weight and a smaller size.

But those photos also show that the B-21 design may not incorporate some of the features that were added to the B-2 to improve low-altitude penetration capability back in the 1980s, most notably the characteristic saw tooth trailing edge design. A less-complex wing design may provide the B-21 with better high-altitude performance and reduce production costs.

Additionally, the photos show the B-21 design includes blended engine nacelles and nearly-flush engine intakes, features that are desirable for stealth, although their

This image shows close-up detailing of the B-21's nose and forward fuselage section, not least its form around the cockpit. US Air Force

incorporation has been limited by difficulties in assuring airflow and in the cost of fabrication.

One fact that has emerged about the B-21 involves the intake and exhaust designs. They proved challenging according to Rob Wittman, Republican-Virginia, and ranking member with the House Armed Services' Seapower and Projection Forces Subcommittee. When speaking to reporters after a speech at the McAleese-Credit Suisse defence conference held in Washington on March 6, 2018, Wittman said: "This is a very, very different design [to the B-2] as far as airflow, and there have been some design challenges there."

The B-21 may also benefit from improvements in fabrication and production technologies. For example, Boeing's MQ-25 Stingray unmanned aerial vehicle tanker for the US Navy has a flush air inlet design, even

though its requirement documents did not call for stealth but did specify the minimisation of production and sustainment costs. New technologies make the use of such design elements less expensive, in both design time and cost terms.

Previously referred to as the Long-Range Strike-Bomber, the B-21 Raider is a new, high-tech long-range bomber that will replace B-1 and B-2 bombers. The B-21 will be a key component of the joint portfolio of conventional and nuclear capable deep-strike capabilities.

B-21 aircraft will be delivered to Ellsworth, Dyess and Whiteman in the mid-2020s. The aircraft is being designed as dual capable, with the ability to employ nuclear weapons, per congressional direction, not later than two years after conventional IOC. The B-21 programme is exploring opportunities to achieve nuclear certification at the earliest

"Highly survivable, the B-21 Raider will have the ability to penetrate modern air defences."

opportunity. Highly survivable, the B-21 Raider will have the ability to penetrate modern air defences.

According to the US Air Force, the B-21's mission is to "Destroy strategic targets to debilitate an adversary's capacity and capability to wage war. The B-21 will maintain the capability to operate in contested environments, counter emerging threats, and support the nuclear triad by providing a visible and flexible nuclear deterrent capability." Additional details of the B-21 are currently classified.

The B-21's FY2023 programme is continuing with the Engineering and Manufacturing Development of the aircraft.

In March 2023, the Secretary of the Air Force Public Affairs office released two new photos from different sight angles to those released at the time of the B-21's unveiling on December 2, 2022. One of the new

images provided close-up detailing of the aircraft's nose and forward fuselage section, not least its form around the cockpit. The second was a partial planform which showed proportions smaller than those of the legacy B-2 Spirit.

Details shown include the deeply-recessed air inlets designed for any-aspect low observability, humps positioned forward of the inlet lip intended to separate turbulent air and prevent entry to the inlet, and a very shallow fuselage form housing the engine nacelles running to the aft of the aircraft.

The planform photo also shows various apertures: two large examples atop each nacelle hump, more apertures of trapezoidal form at the very aft area of the nacelle hump, and others atop the left wing, most likely housing conformal antennae arrays.

The almost white tone of the aircraft's skin appears to be a composite type of material, mostly likely incorporated to ease the maintenance time of the aircraft's low-observable system.

In his keynote address to the Air Force Association Warfare Symposium on March 7, 2023 Secretary of the Air Force Frank Kendall said: "The B-21, which we rolled out just a few months ago, will be the centrepiece of our global strike family of systems. The B-21 is projected to begin flight tests later this calendar year. Our goal is to get into production as quickly as possible with acceptable concurrency risk associated with overlapping some testing with production. With the Congress support, we intend to pursue other capabilities, some defined because of the operational imperative work, that will enhance both the survivability and effectiveness of the B-21."

Airmen repair a B-52H TF33 engine at Andersen Air Force Base, Guam. US Air Force/Senior Airman Jovante Johnson

Each of the B-52H's eight Pratt & Whitney TF33-P-3 turbofan engines provides up to 17,000lb of thrust. Together they can take the aircraft up to 650mph (Mach 0.86) and power the USAF's main strike bomber on a round trip of almost 9,000 miles.

The low-pressure compressor consists of a compressor and fan assembly. The first and second stage rotor blades are longer than those of the remaining stages of the compressor and comprise the fan portion of the turbofan engine.

Take-off rated thrust is obtained by adjusting the throttles to a predetermined value of engine pressure ration (EPR) as determined from a take-off rated thrust EPR curve for the prevailing conditions of field barometric pressure and runway temperature. At ambient temperatures below 100oF (38oC), take-off rated thrust will be obtained at throttle settings below the full forward position.

The eight engines are mounted in pairs in four nacelles suspended below the wings and are numbered in the conventional manner from left to right 1 through 8. The nacelles are also numbered in this manner with engines 1 and 2 in No.1 nacelle, engines 3 and 4 in No.2 nacelle, engines 5 and 6 in No.3 nacelle, and engines 7 and 8 in No.4 nacelle.

In each nacelle pod, diametrically-shaped fin exhaust air ducts are located outboard around each engine and inboard between engines below the strut structure from which the engines are suspended. The nacelle pod cowling is attached to the engine and strut structure by a series

Airmen repair a B-52H engine pylon at Andersen Air Force Base, Guam. The crane was used to lower the TF33 engine from its mounts on the pylon. US Air Force/Senior Airman Jovante Johnson

B-52H Power

Details of the Pratt & Whitney TF33-P-3 turbofan engine, powerplant of the B-52 Stratofortress.

of hooks, pins, and quick-release latches to provide easy access to the engines.

A cowling for each nacelle pod consists of a nose cowl for each engine, a left and right upper and lower wrap cowl, and a left and right upper and lower afterbody cowl. The wrap cowling covers the fan case and a portion of the turbofan exit ducts.

The afterbody cowling covers the engine accessories and the remainder of the engine from the fan bypass duct exit to the aft end of the tailpipe. Airflow from the engine fan exit ducts is discharged axially over the afterbody cowling.

Openings are provided in the cowling for servicing and to facilitate maintenance. The nose cowl, together with the nose dome, forms the engine air inlet.

Eight auxiliary air inlet doors are provided in the cowl to allow a sufficient volume of air to enter the engine during ground operation and take-off.

The doors, which are spring-loaded to the closed position, are opened by differential pressure. Mach number, engine thrust setting, and aircraft angle of-attack determine the differential pressure felt by each door. During ground operation, the doors open because of the pressure across them and assist in producing a more uniform pressure at the engine inlet. For usual flight operation, the doors close during the initial portion of climb and remain closed until landing pattern manoeuvres.

The engines are identical with the exception of the installation of engine-mounted accessories. The accessories are driven from an engine accessories gearbox by means of a shaft which is mechanically geared directly to the main shaft connecting the first stage turbine to the high-pressure compressor.

An airman repairs a B-52H engine pylon.
US Air Force/Senior Airman Jovante Johnson

A 120 KVA generator is installed in a lower centre position of engines 1, 3, 5, and 7. Generator rpm is maintained by use of a constant speed hydraulic drive installed on the same engines. A constant speed drive air-oil cooler is located aft of the generator in the turbofan exit duct where engine fan air used for cooling is exhausted overboard.

Fan air is diverted into special ducts for cooling of the 120 KVA generators and is exhausted overboard from under the afterbody cowl. An engine driven variable delivery hydraulic pump is installed on the lower right side of engines 1, 3, 4, 5, 6, and 7.

An electrically controlled air-drive starter is installed on the lower side of each engine, but the engines have cartridge start capability too. The accessory drive gearbox is also used for mounting the accessories necessary for engine control such as the engine fuel pump, hydromechanical fuel control unit, tachometer generator, and oil pressure transmitter.

ENGINE AIR BLEED
Pneumatic power is provided for engine starting, control cabin air conditioning, anti-icing of the left-wing air-conditioning ram air

A B-52H pilot inspects the TF33 engines of a B-52H in preparation for a flight during a Bomber Task Force deployment to RAF Fairford, England. The aircart hose is used to start only one engine which in turn starts the rest of the engines on the aircraft. US Air Force/Airman 1st Class Duncan Bevan

"An electrically controlled air-drive starter is installed on the lower side of each engine, but the engines have cartridge start capability too."

scoop, and pressurisation of the hydraulic systems reservoirs.

Pneumatics use high-pressure compressor bleed air which is taken directly from the main manifold of the pneumatic system, 16th stage engine bleed air is also used for pressurisation of the constant speed generator drives and the oil tank for each drive.

Operation of the engine bleed valve actuators allows bleeding of the ninth stage low compressor pressure (for prevention of hung starts and engine stall), and for anti-icing of engine nacelle cowls, inlet guide vanes, nose domes, and inlet pitot tubes for the engine pressure ratio (EPR) transducers.

In addition to the use of engine bleed air, turbofan discharge air is used for generator cooling and constant speed drive oil cooling. Bleed air obtained from the body manifold is regulated for pressurisation of the missile environmental system air ducts. Right body manifold bleed air is used for anti-icing of the missile ram air scoop located in the leading edge of the right wing.

ENGINE FUEL CONTROL SYSTEM

An engine fuel control system on each engine automatically provides optimum engine performance for any throttle setting.

The system makes it unnecessary to make throttle adjustments to compensate for variations in inlet temperature, altitude, or airspeed. Fuel from the tanks is routed through the fuel supply system to fuel control units which meter fuel to each engine.

The throttle provides basic engine thrust control and operates through the fuel control unit to position a throttle valve. Engine fuel from the fuel supply system is also controlled by an electrically operated firewall fuel shutoff valve. Power to open this valve is supplied by the fire shutoff switch when the throttles are moved from the closed position. This allows fuel under boost pump pressure to reach a two-stage engine-driven fuel pump. A bypass valve is provided to allow fuel to bypass the first pump stage in the event of failure. Output from the pump is delivered to the fuel control unit.

THROTTLES

Eight throttles on the aisle stand control the firewall fuel shutoff valves and the throttle valves. The throttle quadrant is marked CLOSED-IDLE-OPEN. In the closed position, essential dc power is supplied to close the firewall fuel shutoff valves. Advancing the throttles out of the closed position provides power to open the firewall fuel shutoff valves provided the fire shutoff switches have not been pulled. At the same time, provided the engine starter switch is in start position, essential dc power is supplied to the engine ignition circuit.

"Fuel from the tanks is routed through the fuel supply system to fuel control units which meter fuel to each engine."

SUBSCRIBE TO FAVOURITE MA

YOUR GAZINE

B-52 Landing Gears

Details of the B-52 landing gear system.

A B-52H Stratofortress being lifted off the ground to replace one of its tyres, a process that takes over two hours. US Air Force/Airman Jesse Jenny

A B-52H Stratofortress sits on the flightline during Global Thunder 23 at Minot Air Force Base, North Dakota, April 11, 2023. US Air Force/Senior Airman China Shock

The B-52's landing gear system comprises four two-wheel bogies (the main landing gear) situated under the fuselage and a single outrigger wheel towards the end of each wing. All landing gear are hydraulically actuated through electrically operated valves.

The dual wheel main landing gear are in a quadricycle arrangement with two side by side forward and two side by side rear. The left forward and left rear gear retract forward into fuselage wheel wells while the right forward and right rear gear retract aft into fuselage wheel wells.

The main landing gear doors are mechanically linked to the main landing gear and follow the cycle of operation selected by the normal landing gear lever or the landing gear emergency switches.

The tip gears (outriggers) are located between the outboard engine strut and the external tank strut and retract inboard and slightly forward into each wing. The function of the tip gear is to prevent damage to the wingtips during abnormal ground manoeuvres and/or high gross weight conditions. Normally, the tip gear tyres contact the ground only under maximum weight conditions. The tip gear doors are in two sections.

The strut section is connected to the tip gear and follows the cycle of operation for the gear. The wheel well section is hydraulically actuated and is controlled for proper sequence operation by mechanical linkage in the tip gear system.

Retraction and extension of each landing gear is accomplished by its hydraulic actuator with pressure supplied from the right and left body hydraulic systems.

www.key.aero

A B-52H Stratofortress takes off from Andersen Air Force Base, Guam. US Air Force/Senior Airman Jonathan Ramos

"Normally, the tip gear tyres contact the ground only under maximum weight conditions."

The landing gear is fully retracted in 10 to 15 seconds or extended in 15 to 20 seconds. A single mechanical lock on the main landing gear drag strut locks the main landing gear in either the extended or the retracted position. Oleo safety switches prevent inadvertent gear retraction on the ground. There are no provisions for overriding these switches in an emergency.

LANDING GEAR GROUND LOCKS
Three pairs of landing gear ground locks prevent retraction of the landing gear on the ground. Each ground lock is a pin-type lock with a red warning streamer attached. The tip gear locks are the smallest of the two types. The front main gear locks have the ground lock pin on one end of the streamer and a two-pin steering valve bypass key on the other end. Most rear main gear also have bypass key facilities for use by maintenance when towing from the rear is required. The ground lock pins are inserted in each main landing gear drag strut and each tip gear side brace. The locks are stowed in containers which are located beneath the left equipment rack in the aft end of the navigators' compartment.

MAIN LANDING GEAR SYSTEM
The main landing gear system uses power for operation from the left and right body hydraulic systems which receive main pump pressure from the engine-driven pumps installed on engine No.4 and No.5, respectively. Pressure for actuation of front and aft landing gear which are located on one side of the aircraft is normally supplied from the body system on that same side of the aircraft.

Normal extension or retraction of the main landing gear is accomplished by positioning of the landing gear control lever. An emergency source of pressure is provided which allows separate control of the landing gear by individual switches.

Emergency pressure is provided by connecting the pressure sources of the body

systems to solenoid-operated control valves which are installed on the opposite side of the aircraft.

Each main landing gear may be actuated by either of two solenoid-operated control valves, one of which is supplied with normal system pressure and the other with emergency system pressure. Although separate switches are used for emergency actuation, the emergency system pressure sources of each side's front and aft landing gear are the same as the normal system pressure sources of the opposite front and aft landing gear.

Each of the body systems is equipped with an electric standby pump which is energised by a separate standby pump switch. Standby pump pressure may be supplied as an alternate source of normal system pressure when the engine-driven pumps are not operating or not providing sufficient normal pressure.

Standby pump pressure may be used for actuating the front or aft pair of landing gears separately from the other pair when the engine-driven pumps are not operating. Due to the location of a check valve, pressure from the left body system standby pump is not supplied to the aft landing gear.

Similarly, pressure is not supplied to the forward gear from the right body system standby pump. When the landing gear control lever is positioned, pressure from the left body system standby pump will actuate the forward landing gear through the left normal pressure control valve and the right emergency pressure control valve; pressure from the right body system standby pump will actuate the rear landing gear through the right normal pressure control valve and the left emergency pressure control valve.

The normal gear up circuit supplies power to the crosswind crab cantering motor through switches that centre them to ensure cantering of the main landing gear prior to retraction. This circuit also includes oleo safety switches which prevent inadvertent retraction when either the

left front or right rear main landing gear is on the ground and the oleo strut is compressed more than 0.75in. A gear up lock switch de-energises the circuits when the gear is up and locked. After being unlocked by hydraulic pressure, the landing gear will freefall almost to the down and locked position; therefore, a position switch is included in the circuit. This switch keeps the circuit energised until the landing gear reaches the full down and locked position.

The emergency gear up circuits include oleo safety switches to prevent retraction when either the right front or left rear main landing gear are on the ground. Actuation of the emergency landing gear switches does not automatically centre the landing gear. Each landing gear emergency retract or extend circuit remains energised until the individual emergency switches are placed in the off position.

When the aircraft is on the ground, the landing gear struts are compressed actuating the oleo safety switches. The oleo safety switches are also actuated in flight when the gear is extended and crabbed to an angle equal to or exceeding 14° through any combination of crosswind crab setting and rudder pedal movement.

TIP GEAR SYSTEM
The tip gear system for each gear receives normal hydraulic pressure from the outboard wing hydraulic system. Normal system pressure to the left and right outboard wing hydraulic systems is supplied by engine-driven pumps installed on engine No.1 and No.7, respectively.

Each outboard wing hydraulic system includes an electric standby pump which provides an alternate source of normal system pressure when energised by an individual switch.

Emergency pressure for tip gear extension is provided by the inboard wing hydraulic systems which receive pressure from engine-driven pumps installed on engine No.3 and No.6.

Emergency tip gear extension is accomplished by actuating individual switches

60

which are grouped with the emergency switches for the main landing gear. There are no provisions for emergency retraction.

The tip gear system operates in an indirect manner. In gear down operation, the normal landing gear lever actuates switches which energise the down circuit.

When the solenoid in the normal control valve is energised, hydraulic pressure is directed to the wheel well door actuator and to the normal sequence valve. When the wheel well door opens, mechanical linkage opens the normal sequence valve permitting hydraulic pressure to enter the tip gear actuator thus extending the tip gear. A reverse sequence ensures proper door and gear timing during the retraction cycle. The tip gear circuits pass through the main landing gear oleo safety switches to prevent inadvertent retraction on the ground.

STEERING AND CROSSWIND CRAB SYSTEMS

A means of steering the aircraft on the ground and of pre-setting the crab angle of the landing gear during crosswind landings and take-offs is furnished by two separate yet integrated systems known as the steering and the crosswind crab system. These are integrated through mechanical and cable linkage to a differential coordinating unit. Cable and mechanical linkage from this unit operate steering metering valves on both forward and rear main gear. The steering metering valves meter hydraulic pressure to the actuating cylinders which position each forward gear for steering or all four gears for crosswind crab.

Both the front and rear bogies of the B-52 can be set at angles to either side of the straight-ahead position. Consequently, in a crosswind landing or take-off the aircraft can be headed directly into the wind while rolling down a runway not in line with the wind.

The forward main landing gears are steered by hydraulic pressure controlled by movement of the rudder pedals. The left forward gear

uses pressure from the left body hydraulic system and the right forward gear uses pressure from the right body hydraulic system. An emergency source of hydraulic pressure is not available for steering; however, under certain conditions, standby pressure can be used. In the event of steering failure on one front gear, it will trail the other front gear which has steering available. Only the front

> ## "In a crosswind landing or take-off the aircraft can be headed directly into the wind while rolling down a runway not in line with the wind."

bogies are used for steering the aircraft on the ground.

Steering is accomplished when the rudder pedals move mechanical and cable linkage through a ratio selector unit and a differential coordinating unit to the metering valves which hydraulically position the forward main gear. The steering ratio selector unit mechanically limits steering angles for two conditions. A taxi ratio allows the forward gear to be turned to a maximum angle of 55° right or left of a centre position with full rudder pedal travel.

The second ratio is used for take-off and landing, and restricts the turning angle to approximately 12° right or left of centre. The differential coordinating unit has three main components, a forward drum, a jackscrew, and a rear drum. All three are interconnected. Rudder pedal movement for steering mechanically moves the forward drum in an amount determined by the ratio selector.

Movement of the forward drum moves the rear drum through linkage to mechanically operate the steering metering valves on each of the forward main gear. These valves meter hydraulic pressure to the actuating cylinders to position the gear as desired.

During forward towing operations, a valve between the steering actuating cylinders on each forward gear must be opened by a steering bypass key to bleed pressure. This is to prevent damage caused by hydraulic locking of the pistons in the actuating cylinders. This valve was also incorporated on the rear gear so that towing from the rear could be accomplished.

The bypass keys for the forward gears are attached to the ground lock streamers. When the key is inserted into the steering metering valve receptacle, one pin secures the key in place and the other moves the bypass valve to bleed pressure. Cantering springs are provided near each steering valve which only assist in returning the gear and rudder pedals to neutral whenever pressure on the rudder pedals is removed.

WHEEL BRAKE SYSTEM

Each wheel of the main landing gear has hydraulic brakes. The brakes are of the segmented rotor multiple-disc type using cerametallic brake linings. Braking is accomplished by toe pressure on any or all the rudder pedals. No differential braking is provided. An antiskid system to automatically detect and correct a skid condition is on each wheel of the main landing gear and parking brakes are also provided.

DRAG CUTE SYSTEM

A 44ft ribbon-type drag chute is provided for deceleration during the landing roll. The parachute is installed in a compartment aft of the rudder in the top of the tail section of the fuselage. When the compartment door is opened, the drag chute is deployed. The opening door pulls the ripcord and releases the spring-loaded pilot chute into the slipstream. The pilot chute then pulls out the main drag chute. The risers of the main chute are attached to the aircraft through a terminal held by the jettison mechanism.

A B-52H Stratofortress deployed from Barksdale Air Force Base, Louisiana, takes-off from Andersen Air Force Base, Guam, in support of a Bomber Task Force deployment. US Air Force/Senior Airman Jacob Thompson

Sunrise at Minot Air Force Base, North Dakota. US Air Force/Airman 1st Class Alexander Nottingham

B-52 Systems

Details of the systems and sub-systems of the B-52H Stratofortress heavy bomber aircraft.

The Boeing B-52H Stratofortress is a heavy bomber designed for long range flight at high speed and altitude. The tactical mission is the destruction of surface objectives by bombs and missiles. The aircraft has provisions for ten crew members: a basic crew of five, three instructors and two additional crew members.

The basic crew consists of pilot, co-pilot, radar navigator, navigator, and electronic warfare officer. The instructor crew includes an instructor pilot, instructor navigator and instructor electronic warfare officer.

A highly variable weapons load can be carried on external pylons in combination with the original Common Strategic Rotary Launcher (CSRL) mounted weapons loads.

The CSRL could carry up to eight AGM-86C, B-61, or B-83 weapons internally. These weapon loads cannot be mixed on the CSRL.

Another type of launcher, the Conventional Rotary Launcher can carry a selection of different conventional smart weapons or GPS guided weapons with eight powered up at once.

Externally, the B-52 can suspend weapons using an AGM-28 pylon under each wing with standard rack adapter beams attached to each pylon and two sets of multiple ejector racks (MER) giving a total external carriage capability of 24 weapons. The heavy stores adapter beam (HSAB) can be attached to a stub pylon and up to nine MAU-12 bomb racks can be attached to each HSAB for a total external carriage capability on the HSAB of up to 18 weapons.

SPECIAL FEATURES

The aircraft is characterised by swept wings and empennage, four underslung nacelles housing eight turbofan engines, a quadricycle main landing gear, and a tip gear or outrigger wheel near each outboard engine nacelle.

Engine bleed air provides the air supply for air conditioning and anti-icing. Cartridge starters are installed to provide for engine starts without assistance from an auxiliary air cart or auxiliary electrical power cart.

Primary electrical power is 205-volt ac and is provided by four engine-driven generators.

Hydraulic pressure is supplied by six engine driven hydraulic pumps and two electric motor driven hydraulic pumps.

Primary pitch and yaw control is maintained by hydraulically actuated rudder and elevators. Lateral control is maintained by operation of hydraulically actuated spoilers. By varying the method of control, these same spoilers serve as airbrakes. The entire horizontal stabiliser is moved by a hydraulic mechanism to provide pitch trim. A steering and crosswind crab system provides steering of the forward main landing gear and properly positions both forward and rear main landing gear for crosswind landings.

A hydraulically driven revolver-type launcher installation in the bomb bay provides umbilical and ejector rack connections for the weapons which may be launched/released automatically or manually by the navigators.

The weapon/missile equipment interfaces with the ASQ-176 offensive avionics system (OAS), APN-224 radar altimeter, and the aircraft electrical, bleed air, and body hydraulic systems.

"The Conventional Rotary Launcher can carry a selection of different conventional smart weapons or GPS guided weapons with eight powered up at once."

Weapon selective jettison capability is available to the navigator and radar navigator. The pilot is provided with an ejector unlock consent switch and a pre-arm consent switch (cooperative with the weapons control panel on the navigators' front panel), a launcher hydraulic system selector switch, and a bomb bay and missile jettison control which will jettison all weapons from the aircraft. The pilot is also provided with pylon jettison switches and pylon jettison consent switches. The radar navigator is provided with a bomb bay and missile jettison switch, which will jettison only conventional gravity weapons. This switch is inoperative for all CSRL gravity weapons and all nuclear and conventional missiles.

ESCAPE SYSTEMS

The aircraft escape systems use ejection seats. Ejection seat systems, with their automatic features, increase the airspeed and the high and low extremes of altitude at which safe bale out can be accomplished.

Automatic operation of a system includes stowing the control column, jettisoning the hatch, ejecting the seat, deployment of a drogue parachute, releasing the occupant from the seat, and activating the automatic parachute opening device.

The downward ejection seat systems and the electronic warfare and gunner seats also provide automatic controlled man-seat separation. Release from the seat and opening the parachute can be accomplished manually by overriding the automatic system. However, fully automatic operation greatly reduces the time required for seat separation and chute deployment at low altitudes and makes safe descent from high altitudes possible even if a loss of consciousness occurs.

UPWARD EJECTION SEATS

The pilots' positions in the crew compartment are equipped with forward-facing bucket-type ejection seats designed to provide a safe and effective means of bale out from the aircraft. Provisions are made to accommodate a survival kit and back-type automatic opening parachute and integrated harness.

The electronic warfare officer and gunner are provided with upward ejection seats. The seats are located at the aft of the upper deck and face to the rear of the aircraft. The seat controls are operated in the same manner as the pilot's and co-pilot's seat controls. The sequence of operation of the seat ejection system is the same as the pilots', except for having no control column stowage thruster and having a man-seat separator.

DOWNWARD EJECTION SEATS

The navigator and radar navigator are provided with forward facing downward ejection seats. Each seat is positioned over an escape hatch and has fixed ejection rails. The ejection trigger ring initiates the ejection cycle. One continuous pull on the ejection trigger ring will sequence a series of ballistic devices and mechanical linkages incorporated in the seat to rotate the leg guards, lock the inertia reel, stow the writing table, jettison the hatch, and fire the catapult to eject the seat from the aircraft. The seat is equipped with a drogue parachute and deployment mechanism to positively separate the seat from the seat occupant after the seat leaves the rails. The parachute is in a container mounted below the seat on spring-loaded swinging arms. As the seat leaves the rails, the

A B-52H with a conventional rotary launcher installed in its bomb bay. The CRL allows the B-52 to carry more smart bombs. US Air National Guard/SSgt Patrick Evenson

arms and container swing aft of the seat and deploy the drogue parachute, thus separating the seat from the occupant. Restraint straps connected to the arms to limit travel are interconnected with the integrated harness mechanism to mechanically release the parachute and safety belt fittings as the arms are deployed. These actions are fully automatic and require no action on the part of the crew member.

BOMB DOOR SYSTEM

The bomb door system comprises doors, latches, and the systems which control them. Six double-panel doors cover the bomb bay opening.

All actuation by the bomb door system affects the lower panels only. The upper panels are hinged to provide a larger opening for ground service. The doors are latched at the forward and aft bulkheads of the bomb bay. To secure simultaneous action of all doors, the centre doors are mechanically linked to the forward and aft doors.

The doors can be operated with the bomb door switch on either the pilot's or radar navigator's control panel. The OAS can operate the doors automatically. The bomb or missile jettison systems will open the doors but will not close them.

During ground operation, with no power on the aircraft, the bomb doors may be unlatched

by manually pulling the bomb door latch release cable in the aft wheel well. The bomb doors are held closed by mechanical latches and held open by hydraulic pressure. The right body hydraulic system supplies normal pressure to operate the forward and aft bomb door actuators through the forward and aft main control valves. The left body hydraulic system supplies alternate pressure automatically to the forward bomb door actuator through the forward emergency control valve whenever the normal pressure is low or fails.

The forward bomb door latch actuator is supplied normal pressure by the left body hydraulic system through the forward emergency control valve. The aft bomb door

> *"The pilots' positions in the crew compartment are equipped with forward-facing bucket-type ejection seats designed to provide a safe and effective means of bale out."*

The OAS controls power application, programming, and release of weapons. The OAS also provides signal processing, storage avionics, control and display panels, weapon supervision, regulated dc power conversion, and monitors environmental control equipment in the aircraft. The OAS interfaces with the carrier electrical sources and panel lighting.

Primary weapon control and monitor is provided through the OAS weapon control panel (WCP), integrated keyboard (IKB) and the multifunction displays (MFD).

The B-52, when configured for JSOW carriage and release, is equipped with ICSMS OAS hardware and software, including the JSOW stores management overlay (SMO).

JOINT STAND-OFF WEAPON (JSOW)

JSOW is an air-to-ground glide weapon that provides a standoff outside of point defence capability against a variety of land and sea targets. The weapon can be delivered in several variants, each of which uses a common weapon body and substitute various payloads.

The weapon consists of an aerodynamically efficient airframe with folding wings and non-folding fixed and movable tail surfaces. With wings folded and suspended by standard 30in suspension lugs, JSOW size and weight allow carriage on external stations. The weapon is stored and loaded as a fully assembled, all-up round.

JSOWs are carried externally on common pylon assemblies which are attached to the wing pylon adapter. Up to six JSOWs can be carried on each common pylon which comprises a stub pylon (which are modified wing pylons), a Heavy Stores Adapter Beam (HSAB), and MAU-12 ejector racks.

B-52/JDAM WEAPON SYSTEM

The B-52 JDAM weapon system consists of a Conventional Enhancement Modification (CEM) modified B-52 with OAS, including a GPS, and the Joint Direct Attack Munition (JDAM). The aircraft has the capability of carrying multiple JDAM weapons.

The JDAM is a launch and leave low drag bomb autonomously guided by an onboard GPS-aided Inertial Navigation System.

The OAS controls power application, programming, and release of weapons, and provides signal processing, storage avionics, control and display panels, weapon supervision, regulated dc power conversion, and monitors environmental control equipment in the aircraft.

Primary weapon control and monitor is provided through the OAS weapon control panel (WCP), integrated keyboard (IKB) and the multifunction displays (MFD).

JDAM weapons are carried externally on modified weapon suspension assemblies which are attached to the wing pylon adapter. Up to six JDAM weapons can be carried on each wing pylon although JDAM types

latch actuator is supplied normal pressure by the right body hydraulic system through the aft main control valve. Neither the forward nor aft bomb door latch actuator has an alternate source of hydraulic pressure.

Both bomb door latch actuators are bussed together by cable so that when hydraulic pressure is available to either or both bomb door latch actuators, the forward and aft latches will be released.

A forward special weapon manual release handle is connected to the latch actuator cable to provide an emergency means of unlatching the bomb doors. Air loads will then position the bomb doors to some position between closed and full open depending on

indicated airspeed. Bomb door operation is computer controlled for launch or normal jettison of bomb bay missiles. During the computer-controlled bomb door open phase, the bomb door safety relay is energised and disables all bomb-door-close circuits.

B-52/JSOW SYSTEM

The B-52 JSOW system consists of a Conventional Enhancement Modification (CEM) modified B-52 with OAS, including a -46 GPS, and the Joint Standoff Weapon (JSOW).

The B-52 has the capability of releasing 12 JSOWs, six from each Heavy Stores Adapter Beam (HSAB) mounted on an ICSMS external pylon.

JDAMs loaded on a conventional rotary launcher installed in a B-52H's bomb bay.
US Air National Guard/SSgt Patrick Evenson

cannot be mixed on a pylon. Each suspension assembly consists of a stub pylon (which are modified wing pylons), a Heavy Stores Adapter Beam (HSAB), and MAU-12 ejector racks.

The free flight state of, for example, the 2,000lb GBU-31 JDAM involves separation from the aircraft, fuse arming, GPS satellite acquisition, guidance optimisation, terminal trajectory adjustment and target impact. This state begins at the successful completion of the launch state. A JDAM's flight consists of three phases - separation, optimal guidance, and impact.

SEPARATION PHASE

The weapon is released with the fins locked to prevent any control actions which could jeopardise safe separation from the host aircraft. The fins remain locked for one second after release. After the one second delay, the fins are unlocked, electrical power from the initiator is applied to the fuse and the autopilot provides fin commands to damp angular rates and control the weapon to the desired flight attitude.

The Mk84 JDAM rolls to the desired flight attitude of a + configuration with the fixed fin down and the suspension lugs at approximately a 45° angle. The BLU-109 JDAM remains in an X configuration after separation with the fixed fin up and to the left and the suspension lugs straight up.

For both variants, the guidance acceleration commands to the autopilot are phased in during the first 250 msec after the fins are unlocked.

OPTIMAL GUIDANCE PHASE

The optimal guidance flight phase takes place from the completion of the separation phase, when full guidance authority is achieved, until

> ## "Bomb door operation is computer controlled for launch or normal jettison of bomb bay missiles."

the impact phase. The optimal guidance phase includes the acquisition of the GPS flight process, which starts three seconds after release so that the weapon is not shadowed by the aircraft and to minimise the possibility of receiving multipath GPS signals.

The optimal guidance law computes, in real time, the minimal control effort (manoeuvres) to go from the present position and velocity state to impacting the target at the desired flight path and approach angle. These computations are continuously made throughout the optimal guidance phase and the resulting acceleration commands are executed by the weapon's autopilot. This optimal guidance law is used for both horizontal and vertical targets with level, dive, loft and toss release conditions.

The guidance law continually computes the optimal weapon trajectory from its current position to the target, to achieve an impact vector at the planned impact point, with the planned impact angle, impact azimuth, and minimum velocity. If all planned impact conditions are not achievable, the guidance law trades off impact velocity first, then impact angle/azimuth and finally impact point.

As the weapon nears its target, it will roll 180° and pull down on the target to align its angle

of attack with its velocity vector. For horizontal targets, this pull-down results in a steep descent to maximize warhead penetration and to improve fuse and warhead reliability. For vertical targets, the weapon performs the same roll and pull-down manoeuvre, but the resulting descent may not be as steep. Again, the proper descent angle for both types of targets is continually computed by the guidance law throughout the weapon's free flight, until it enters the impact phase.

IMPACT PHASE

The impact phase is the last one second of flight, during which the weapon attitude is actively controlled, to zero the total angle of attack. This is done to align the warhead longitudinal axis to the velocity vector to prevent warhead breakup. The navigation system estimates the time to impact and the angle of attack. At one second prior to impact the optimal guidance commands are zeroed and an attitude command equal to the velocity vector orientation is sent to the autopilot. This results in zeroing the weapon's angle of attack before impact.

The resulting descent and minimum angle of attack results in maximum impact velocity for effective penetration of hardened targets.

Airmen from the 5th Maintenance Group work on a B-52H at Minot Air Force Base, North Dakota. US Air Force/Airman 1st Class Heather Ley

"The proper descent angle for both types of targets is continually computed by the guidance law throughout the weapon's free flight."

A B-52H takes off from Diego Garcia on its way to Afghanistan in support of Operation Enduring Freedom in April 2006. US Air Force/SMSgt John Rohrer

B-52H
The Cadillac

Jon Lake details the evolution of the B-52, the final version of the Stratofortress bomber.

> "The B-52H has become the US Air Force's principal long-range, large-payload multi-role strategic bomber, and it operates in both nuclear and conventional roles."

B-1B's hourly flying cost has been calculated at $173,014 per flying hour. Costs quoted are in constant FY2020 dollars. The B-52 also scores highly when it comes to readiness. According to one official report, the B-52 had the highest mission capable rate of the US Air Force's three heavy bomber types, averaging 80.5%. The B-1B had an average mission capable rate of 53.7% while the B-2 Spirit managed only 30.3%.

It is no surprise that the B-52H has become the US Air Force's principal long-range, large-payload multi-role strategic bomber, and it operates in both nuclear and conventional roles.

The B-52H forms a vital component of the United States' strategic nuclear deterrent capabilities, as Zachary Keck explained in his article *Nuclear Bombers in an A2/AD World* in *the Diplomat*. A2/AD is the acronym for Anti-Access/Area Denial, a military strategy employed to control access to and within an operating environment.

Zach made the point that: "the bomber fleet's nuclear missions do not actually include dropping nuclear bombs on enemies. Instead, its main utility for America's nuclear deterrent — including extended deterrent — is to signal to adversaries and reassure allies. America can send its nuclear-capable bombers abroad to signal to adversaries and allies alike. Because of their visibility, bombers are able to achieve this in a way that ICBMs located in the United States and ballistic missile submarines cannot.

"This is an incredibly important mission; in fact, unless something goes terribly wrong, this is the only nuclear mission the US will ever have to carry out. However, if deterrence ever did fail and the US had to carry out a nuclear strike, it would almost certainly not rely on its bomber fleets to do so. America's ICBMs would be the most likely leg of the triad to be used given their combination of accuracy and their ability to penetrate enemy defences."

But while the manned bombers might not be critical in an all-out nuclear exchange, their deterrent value is considerable, and the B-52 also has a real part to play throughout the spectrum of conflict, in a way that ICBMs and SLBMs cannot. In any near-peer conventional conflict, the B-52H would be a decisive and

With a weapons payload of more than 70,000lb, the B-52H can carry the most diverse range of ordnance of any US Air Force combat aircraft. This ability includes the US Air Force's largest conventional bomb, the 30,000lb GBU-57A/B Massive Ordnance Penetrator, as well as a wide range of gravity bombs, laser- and GPS-guided bombs, joint direct attack munitions, cluster bombs, and JASSM-ER precision guided missiles.

The B-52H has an unrefuelled combat range more than 8,800 miles, and the use of air-to-air refuelling gives the aircraft a range that is limited only by aircrew endurance.

According to the US Government Accountability Office *Weapon System Sustainment* report published in November 2022, the B-52H enjoys a higher mission-capable rate than its sisters, and at $88,354 per flying hour is also cheaper to operate than the B-2, which costs $150,741 per hour. The

Crew chiefs prepare a B-52H for take-off at Minot Air Force Base, North Dakota, June 2, 2020, ahead of a long duration Bomber Task Force mission throughout Europe and the Arctic region. US Air Force/Senior Airman Alyssa Day

potent asset, since its long range and ability to carry large numbers of stand-off weapons mean that it can deliver effect while standing back from the most contested and congested parts of the battlespace.

In a conventional campaign, the B-52H can undertake strategic attack, close-air support, air interdiction, offensive counter-air and maritime ocean surveillance, mine-laying, anti-surface vessel and anti-submarine warfare operations.

Today, 76 B-52H bombers are in service, assigned to the 5th Bomb Wing at Minot Air Force Base, North Dakota, and to the 2nd Bomb Wing at Barksdale Air Force Base, Louisiana, both units coming under the control of Air Force Global Strike Command.

The type is also assigned to Air Force Reserve Command's 307th Bomb Wing, also based at Barksdale. Ten more are in storage with the US Air Force's 309th Aerospace Maintenance And Regeneration Group at Davis-Monthan Air Force Base, Arizona, and five are in use as ground test or ground instructional airframes. Ten further aircraft have been lost in accidents, and one has been scrapped, accounting for the 102 aircraft production run.

The B-52 is widely if irreverently known as the BUFF. This originated as a vulgar acronym (standing for Big Ugly Fat F*cker), and was coined after a similar epithet (SLUF, or 'Short Little Ugly F*ucker') was given to its Vietnam War comrade in arms, the A-7 Corsair.

Though we do not intend to set out the entire history of the BUFF here, it is worthwhile briefly outlining how the B-52H came to be.

H-MODEL

The B-52H was the final production version of Boeing's B-52 Stratofortress. The Stratofortress first flew in prototype form on April 15, 1952, and entered service in 1955. This makes the B-52 the longest-serving combat aircraft in the world – and one that is celebrated its 70th anniversary in 2022! Even the youngest B-52H in the fleet (serial number 61-0040) marked 60 years of service on October 26, 2022.

The B-52 designation was originally set aside for a new strategic bomber whose

Crew chiefs prepare to de-ice the windows of a B-52H during an exercise to prepare the 5th Bomb Wing for a conventional operational readiness inspection.
US Air Force/Senior Airman Jesse Lopez

"If deterrence ever did fail and the US had to carry out a nuclear strike, it would almost certainly not rely on its bomber fleets to do so."

desired performance characteristics were set out by the US Army Air Force's Air Materiel Command on November 23, 1945. The aircraft was to be "capable of carrying out the strategic mission without dependence upon advanced and intermediate bases controlled by other countries."

Boeing's Model 462, a straight-winged bomber powered by six Wright T35 turboprops, was declared the winner of the competition, even though it didn't meet some of the specified requirements – being notably deficient in range. As requirements changed, Boeing produced a succession of revised designs (using the Model 464 designation, with numerical suffixes), reducing the overall size of the aircraft, adopting four engines, and

a swept back wing. None of these designs offered a significant improvement over the Convair B-36 Peacemaker, which first flew on August 8, 1946, and the entire project was postponed for six months.

Boeing continued to refine its design, though outright cancellation looked to be on the cards after the Heavy Bombardment Committee was convened to lay down performance requirements for a nuclear bomber In September 1947. The committee's requirements were formally issued on December 8, 1947, with the required top speed of 500 miles per hour and stipulated 8,000-mile range, was out of reach for a turboprop bomber like Boeing's latest 464-29. Boeing president William McPherson Allen told

Secretary of the Air Force Stuart Symington that the company's design could be adapted to incorporate new aviation technologies and thereby meet the more stringent requirements, and in April 1948 presented a $30m proposal for the design, construction, and testing of two Model 464-35 prototypes. Jet engines were added to the design in May 1948, creating the Model 464-40, but the air force favoured the turboprop powered 464-35, and this formed the basis of the proposal submitted to the US Air Force's chief of bomber development, Colonel Pete Warden on Thursday, October 21, 1948, by three Boeing engineers – George S. Schairer, Art Carlsen and Vaughn Blumenthal. Warden was underwhelmed, and asked for a jet proposal, which the Boeing team (joined by the company's vice president for engineering, Ed Wells) worked on overnight in the Hotel van Cleve in Dayton, Ohio, and delivered the following day. On Friday, Col Warden looked over the new proposal and, still unimpressed, asked for a better design.

Returning to their hotel, the Boeing team (joined by Boeing engineers Bob Withington and Maynard Pennell, who were in town on other business) set about creating a new design. This was the Model 464-49 which combined 35° swept wings with eight engines paired in four underwing pods, and which used a B-47-like bicycle landing gear with wingtip outriggers. While the bulk of the team got out their slide rules and worked on weight and performance data, George Schairer set about building a model, after a trip to a hobby shop for supplies, Schairer, and Ed Wells, who was also a skilled artist, completed the aircraft drawings. That Monday, Schairer presented Col Warden with a neatly bound, freshly typed, 33-page proposal and his 14in balsa wood scale model. Warden was finally (almost) satisfied! "Now we have an airplane," he said. "This is the B-52!"

With range still a concern, Boeing scaled up the design to create the larger Model 464-67, which became the XB-52 and YB-52 prototypes. For the production B-52A and subsequent

variants there was one further design change, with Strategic Air Command's commander General Curtiss LeMay's insistence, a switch from B-47 style tandem seating for pilot and co-pilot to a more conventional side-by-side cockpit.

> **"The missile was designed to be launched from a range of 1,000 miles from its target, allowing the launch aircraft to remain well outside the range of Soviet air defences."**

At the B-52A's roll-out ceremony on March 18, 1954, General Nathan Twining, the Air Force Chief of Staff said: "The long rifle was the great weapon of its day. ... today this B-52 is the long rifle of the air age."

Boeing went on to build 449 tall-tailed B-52s, consisting of three B-52As, 50 B-52Bs, 35 B-52Cs, 170 B-52Ds, 100 B-52Es and 89 B-52Fs. In the normal run of events, the B-52 would have been replaced by the Mach 2-capable Convair B-58 Hustler and a production version of the even faster North American XB-70 Valkyrie, but the introduction of surface-to-air missiles by the USSR in the late 1950s removed the sanctuary of high altitude, and the adoption of low-level penetration tactics removed any advantage enjoyed by the putative B-52 replacements. Instead, the B-52 was itself adapted as a

low-level penetration bomber, using terrain masking to avoid detection by radar and thereby negate the radar-guided surface-to-air missile threat. From November 1959, the so-called Big Four modification programme (also known as Modification 1000) saw all but the early B-52A and B-52B models receiving a range of modifications, including AGM-28 Hound Dog standoff nuclear missiles and ADM-20 Quail decoys. Major structural modifications were subsequently embodied in a succession of upgrade packages.

SHORT TAIL

With the Convair B-58 Hustler facing delay (or even cancellation) and with technical obsolescence looming for the US Air Force's strategic bomber force by the early 1960s, Boeing launched the development of a new B-52 variant even before the RB-52B had been declared combat ready. At first, a radical redesign was envisaged with a completely new wing and powered by Pratt & Whitney J75 engines, which would be tested on the XB-52A prototype.

Boeing received $1.2m, and design work began in June 1956, just three months after the RB-52B had entered service. But the advanced B-52 derivative being drawn up was soon cancelled to avoid production delays, and the B-52G became a rather more

A B-52H assigned to the 96th Bomb Squadron based at Barksdale Air Force Base, Louisiana, takes off from Nellis Air Force Base, Nevada.
US Air Force/TSgt Michael Holzworth

modest upgrade of the basic design, though significant changes were implemented.

The aircraft retained the J57-P-43WA engines of the B-52F, though with water capacity increased to 1,200 US gallons, they could use water injection for longer, increasing the time for which 13,750lb would be available, rather than the usual limit of 11,200lb per engine. To leverage greater performance gains, and to compensate for the weight of an increase in internal fuel capacity, Boeing embarked on a massive weight reduction effort, shaving 15,000lb from the aircraft's empty weight.

The B-52G was designed around a new wet wing with three integral fuel tanks, which necessitated a complete structural redesign. The new wing used long new wing skins machined from lighter-weight alloys with integral stiffeners. This gave a minimum number of chordwise joints and this, it was confidently predicted, would reduce the risk of fuel leaks, and would increase fatigue tolerance. Lighter flap drive motors were fitted (though these increased retraction times) and the ailerons were deleted. Roll control on the B-52 had always been achieved primarily by using spoilers. This was due to the risk of wing twist when ailerons were deflected, although older B-52 variants had incorporated small feeler ailerons - primarily to provide feedback to the flying controls.

The elimination of the ailerons increased the tendency of the aircraft to Dutch roll and tended to induce a slight buffet or a nose up pitching moment. This was especially noticeable during air-to-air refuelling contacts, though it was solved via a minor modification.

The new integral tanks took total internal fuel tankage to 46,575 US gal, replacing the rubber bladder-type tanks of the B-52F which had contained 41,553 US gal of fuel. In addition, a pair of 700 US gal external fuel tanks were fitted under the wings on wet hardpoints, though these were fitted more to relieve the bending moment on the wing and to help prevent wing flutter than for additional fuel capacity and were smaller than the 3,000-gallon underwing auxiliary fuel tanks (which could be jettisoned) fitted to the B-52C, B-52D, B-52E and B-52F.

The B-52G's most obvious recognition feature was that its tail fin was reduced in height by eight feet. Because the chord was increased at the same time, the new tail looked much broader and stubbier than the 'witches' hat' design used on previous B-52 versions. The new tail was tested on the first B-52A (52-001). At the other end of the aircraft, the nose radome was enlarged and redesigned, and on the B-52G was of one-piece construction.

Another obvious visible change was the removal of the tail gunner's position in the rear fuselage, at the base of the rudder. The tail gunner was relocated to the cockpit, sitting beside the electronic warfare officer on a rearward-facing upward-firing ejection seat.

This put all six crew members together, with the offensive crew (pilot and co-pilot on the upper deck and the two bombing navigation system operators on the lower deck) facing forward and the defensive crew (tail gunner and ECM operator) on the upper deck facing aft. This was known as the battle station

concept. The seats were redesigned to lessen the fatigue of 20-hour missions.

The remotely operated rear-firing gun turret was aimed using an Avco-Crosley ASG-15 fire control system with separate radar dishes for search and track and initially a television camera, though the latter was subsequently replaced by ALQ-117 countermeasures equipment.

The B-52G made its maiden flight on August 31, 1958, and entered service with the 5th Bomb Wing at Travis Air Force Base, California on February 13, 1959, the day after the last B-36 was retired.

Some 193 B-52Gs were manufactured between October 1958 and February 1961, making the G-model the most numerous Stratofortress variant. It was also the first Stratofortess version to be built exclusively at the Wichita factory, whereas previous variants had been built at both Wichita and Seattle. The change freed up the Seattle plant to concentrate on the production of airliners.

Though the B-52G had a lighter structure than previous versions, it carried more fuel, and had a higher gross weight (38,000lb heavier than the B-52F at 488,000lb).

This combination of lightweight structure and heavy operational weights inevitably led to fatigue problems relatively early in the aircraft's service career. Fatigue cracking was severe enough to require the imposition of stringent flying restrictions, and an urgent package of modifications was embodied.

THE FINAL VERSION

The final production Stratofortress variant was the B-52H, which followed the B-52G on the Wichita production line.

A B-52H con-trailing over North America during an eight-hour sortie flown from Minot Air Force Base, North Dakota. US Air Force/SSgt Andy Kin

The new B-52H was designed as a carrier for the Douglas GAM-87 Skybolt missile – an air-launched ballistic air-to-surface missile that promised to keep Strategic Air Command's manned bombers relevant and viable. The missile was designed to be launched from a range of 1,000 miles from its target, allowing the launch aircraft to remain well outside the range of Soviet air defences. To achieve this the missile used the W59 lightweight thermonuclear warhead from the Minuteman ICBM, in a Mk7 re-entry vehicle. The GAM-87 was powered by a two-stage solid-fuel rocket motor and had eight movable tail fins on the first stage and a gimballed nozzle on the second.

The B-52H could carry four missiles, two under each wing on an inverted-Y dual launcher adapter. When seen in plan view, the Skybolt seeker sections projected ahead of the wing leading edge, allowing the missile's star tracker to continually observe the sky.

As well as attachment points for the Skybolt, the new variant incorporated several other modifications. Between the engine nacelles, the B-52H had small pylons for ALE-25 forward-firing chaff rockets. The aircraft was also fitted with integrated flight instrumentation for improved low-level capabilities, an advanced capability radar with terrain following capabilities and an Emerson ASG-21 fire control system.

Externally, the new version was distinguished by a new tail-armament, with the usual quad 0.50in machine guns giving way to a General Electric M61 20mm Vulcan cannon. Finally, and perhaps most obviously, the B-52's traditional J57 turbojet powerplant gave way to the TF33 turbofan. The new engines had a larger fan/compressor stage than the J57, which required a larger-diameter intake and a bypass air outlet, markedly changing the outline of the engine nacelles.

The Boeing 707 had already demonstrated the advantages conferred by the JT3D (the civil version of the TF33), which included a 13% reduction in specific fuel consumption. This gave the B-52H 20% longer range than

> **"Kennedy cancelled the programme three days later, to the fury of the British, who had been relying on Skybolt for their national nuclear deterrent."**

the G model, as well as lots of excess power. This equated to a 50% increase in take-off thrust (giving a 500ft reduction in take-off ground roll), and a 20% boost in cruise power. The new engine was also quieter and had a more rapid throttle response.

The TF33 was more environmentally friendly than the older J57 and did not leave a thick plume of black smoke. The TF33 did not use water injection, and the deletion of this made it unnecessary to maintain large stocks of distilled water pre-positioned at forward air bases, which had always complicated the rapid deployment of the B-52G and earlier versions.

The new TF33 turbofans were not without some teething troubles. Pilots experienced throttle creep, uneven throttle alignment, hard and reluctant engine starts, excessive oil consumption, turbine blade failures and flameouts. The B-52H was briefly even taken off alert. The Hot Fan programme was launched in mid-1962 to increase the reliability of the TF33 and address these problems. It was completed by the end of 1964.

There was no B-52H prototype, but the TF33 turbofan engines were first tested on B-52G 57-6471 (which was temporarily re-designated as a JB-52G and sometimes referred to as the YB-52H). The first true B-52H flew on July 20, 1960, and production deliveries to operational units began on May 9, 1961.

The last B-52H was delivered to the 4136th Strategic Wing at Minot Air Force Base on October 26, 1962, bringing production of the Stratofortress to an end.

The Skybolt missile for which the B-52H had been optimised never entered service. A decision to proceed with the Skybolt was reached in February 1960, and this was to have led to initial deployment in 1964. The UK joined the project in June 1960, ordering 100 Skybolts for carriage by the Avro Vulcan, though the British planned to use their own Red Snow warhead on safety grounds. Robert McNamara, John F Kennedy's defence secretary from January 21, 1961, was always opposed to Skybolt, and believed that manned bombers were obsolete, and unnecessary in the age of the SLBM and ICBM.

Once the submarine-launched Polaris was in service, with the Minuteman under development, Skybolt started to look a bit superfluous, and poor test results were the final straw. After five failed attempts, the first fully successful flight was made on December 19, 1962. Kennedy cancelled the programme three days later, to the fury of the British, who had been relying on Skybolt for their national nuclear deterrent.

Thereafter, the B-52H relied on the same weapons as earlier variants, principally the AGM-28 Hound Dog and thermonuclear gravity bombs. The B-52G and B-52H thereafter followed similar careers, often receiving the same modifications and upgrades, though the better performance and

B-52H 60-0044 parked on the flight line at Minot Air Force Base, North Dakota, on August 8, 2022. The image shows the wrinkly-looking surface of the aircraft's aluminium skin, a condition caused by buckling that is induced by loading when in flight. US Air Force/Airman Alysa Knott

longer range of the B-52H meant that the high-profile nuclear role was always emphasised, and though the aircraft had conventional capabilities, these were seldom exercised, and the aircraft was not used in Vietnam, for example, though B-52H aircrew were rotated

through theatre to spread the load, flying B-52Ds or B-52Gs.

As a result, the B-52H Wings always had something of a cachet, and pilots enjoyed flying the high-performance BUFF that they called the Cadillac.

Flight operations at Barksdale Air Force Base, Louisiana. US Air Force/TSgt Robert Horstman

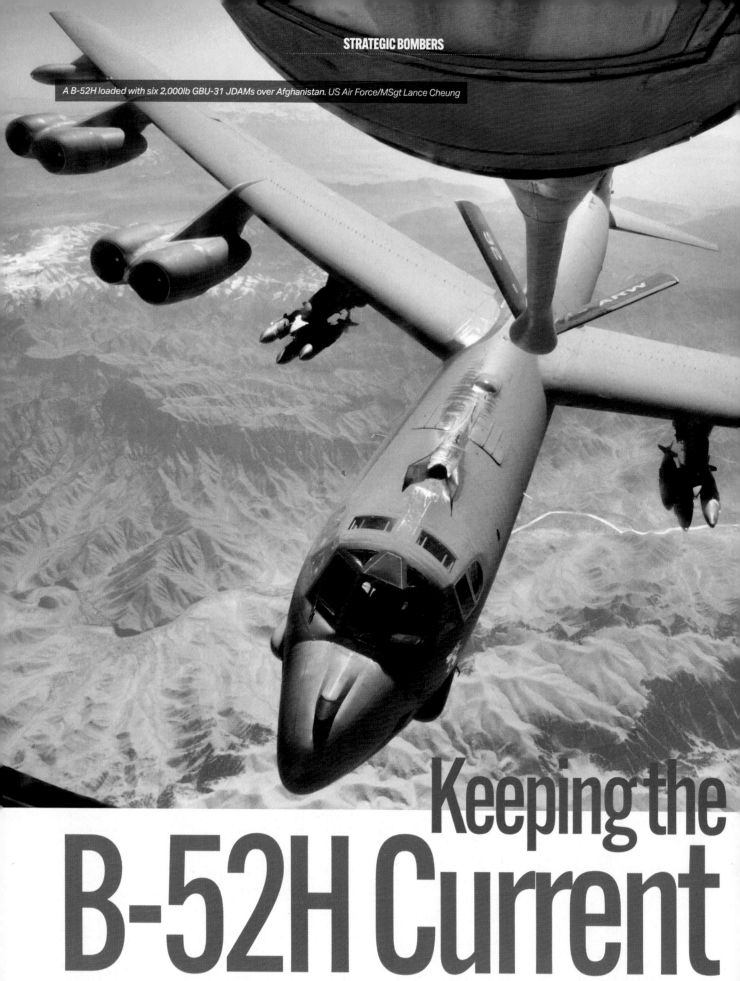

A B-52H loaded with six 2,000lb GBU-31 JDAMs over Afghanistan. US Air Force/MSgt Lance Cheung

Keeping the B-52H Current

Jon Lake details the many upgrade programmes implemented for the B-52H bomber to keep the longest-serving combat aircraft in the world viable.

A B-52H with a Conventional Rotary Launcher installed in the aircraft's weapons bay at Al Udeid Air Base, Qatar, on November 17, 2017. The CRL allows the B-52 to carry more smart bombs.
US Air National Guard/SSgt Patrick Evenson

will continue, so that the B-52H that retires sometime in the 2050s will be a different aeroplane again.

MODIFICATIONS
One early post-Cold War change to the B-52H came in 1992, with the decision to remove the 20mm cannon from the tail and the gunner from the crew. General George L Butler, then head of Strategic Air Command said: "My decision to eliminate the guns from the BUFF was not an easy one. It stemmed from the collapse of the Soviet threat and the leading edge of very sharp budget cuts… Our air force is going to go through a lengthy period of turmoil as we adapt to a dramatically changing world." The tail gunners were reassigned to other duties, and the aircraft were modified as they went through maintenance.

The early 1990s were marked by a drive to improve the conventional capabilities of the B-52H, to compensate for the early retirement of the B-52G-model.

Eight aircraft were modified in 1994 under the Rapid Eight programme, giving four (60-0013, 61-0013, 61-0019 and 61-0024) an interim AGM-84 Harpoon capability, and four (60-0014, 60-0025, 60-0062 and 61-0004) an interim AGM-142 Have Nap capability.

The Conventional Enhancement Modification (CEM) programme gave the B-52H a more comprehensive conventional weapons capability, adding the modified stub underwing weapon pylons used by conventionally armed B-52Gs, as well as full Harpoon and Have Nap integration. The new pylons were able to carry new-generation MIL-STD 1760 weapons, and the offensive avionics system received new stores management overlays for a range of new weapons, including Joint Direct Attack Munitions (JDAMs), Wind Corrected Munitions Dispensers (WCMDs), AGM-154 Joint Stand-off Weapons and AGM-158 Joint Air-to-Surface Stand-off Missiles. The CEM programme also introduced new radios, integrated GPS into the aircraft's navigation system and replaced the under-nose FLIR with a more modern unit. Forty-seven B-52Hs were modified under the CEM

programme by 1996, with 19 more by the end of 1999. The B-52H gained limited initial operational capability for the WCMD and JDAM in December 1998, while JSOW entered service in 2003 and was deployed during Operation Iraqi Freedom, and JASSM was cleared for operational use in October 2003. At much the same time, the B-52 also began using the Litening targeting pod, allowing it to self-designate for laser guided bombs. From 2008, Litening gave way to the Sniper AT targeting pod.

In June 2006, Boeing was awarded a contract for the B-52 smart weapons integration next-generation (SWING) programme, to support the integration of future weapon systems including the JASSM-ER extended-range version, and the small diameter bomb – up to 32 of the latter able to be carried on the common strategic rotary launcher in the bomb bay.

From September 2015, Air Force Global Strike Command began the conversion of a portion of the B-52H bomber fleet from a nuclear to a conventional only capability aircraft under the New Strategic Arms Reduction Treaty (New START). Under the terms of New START the US Department of Defense was to retain just 60 nuclear capable heavy bombers - 19 B-2s and 41 B-52Hs. Thirty B-52H bombers were therefore converted to a conventional only role, so removing them from accountability under the treaty. The 12 non-operational B-52H aircraft in storage with the US Air Force's 309th Aerospace Maintenance And Regeneration Group at Davis-Monthan Air Force Base, Arizona, were also converted to a conventional-only configuration.

With a weapons payload of more than 70,000lb, the B-52H is also capable of carrying an extremely diverse range of weapons, though the CEM modification only allowed carriage of modern smart weapons underwing, and not in the bomb bay, limiting weapons numbers to 12 JDAMs or 16 WCMDs, for example.

WEAPONS CARRIAGE
The B-52 MIL-STD-1760 Internal Weapons Bay Upgrade programme (IWBU) dramatically

hough the B-52H variant has been in service for more than 60 years, the aircraft that equips today's Stratofortress Wings at Barksdale and Minot is a very different beast to the one that entered service with the 379th Bombardment Wing (Heavy) at Wurtsmith Air Force Base, Michigan in May 1961. But today's BUFF is also a very different aircraft to the B-52H that flew the Desert Strike mission in 1995, and even to the B-52Hs that went to war in Iraq in 2003. They might look the same, but a programme of upgrades and modifications have transformed their operational capabilities. That progress is ongoing, and

increased smart weapons capacity by modifying existing Common Strategic Rotary Launchers (CSRLs) into Conventional Rotary launchers (CRLs), allowing them to carry smart weapons inside the bomb bay. The modification used parts from existing rotary launchers, as well as hardware and software already developed for the wing pylons. Some 44 CSRLs were converted into CRLs, including three prototype launchers for test and evaluation. Six were delivered and the CRL achieved initial operational capability in March 2016.

Increment 1.1 allowed the internal carriage of eight JDAMs and variants, to include Laser JDAM (LJDAM), on the rotary launcher. Additionally, this increment allowed the external carriage of 16 LJDAMs. Increment 1.2 allowed the internal carriage of eight AGM-158 Joint Air-to-Surface Standoff Missiles (JASSMs) - including JASSM Extended Range (JASSM-ER) and added external carriage of 12 JASSM-ER missiles. The second increment also allowed the carriage of eight ADM-160 Miniature Air Launched Decoys (MALD) or MALD Jammer (MALD-J) variants.

The bomb bay upgrade also allowed the B-52H to carry all its weapons internally, saving 15% in fuel and hiding weapons carriage from potential adversaries.

Upgrades to the B-52H's weapons bay allowed the force to accelerate its transition from the 1,500-mile range AGM-86C and AGM-86D Conventional Air Launched Cruise Missiles (CALCMs) to the 575-mile range AGM-158B JASSM-ER. The CALCM was retired on November 20, 2019, replaced in the conventional standoff strike role by the AGM-158B. The reduction in range will be mitigated in part when the 1,200-mile range AGM-158D enters service, if it meets its range specifications (see below).

The US Air Force has not neglected the B-52H's external carriage capabilities. The current Improved Common Pylon (ICP) provides both analogue and digital MIL-STD-1760 weapons carriage and release capabilities but was designed in 1959 and cannot carry weapons heavier than 5,000lb. Although it has performed exceptionally well, the weight of new weapons has led to concerns as to its structural integrity, and in 2018, the US Air Force issued a request

for information from defence companies to identify potential sources that may possess the expertise, capabilities, and experience to replace the existing external heavy weapons delivery system. Air Force Materiel Command is seeking a new external weapons pylon that will take the B-52H's current 10,000lb maximum external load (spread across two underwing pylons) to 40,000lb. The new pylon would enable the B-52H to carry any of the air-launched munitions in the US Air Force inventory including the 22,000lb GBU-43/A Massive Ordnance Air Burst (MOAB) bomb, known colloquially as the Mother Of All Bombs.

CRUISE MISSILES
Arguably the most urgent requirement for the B-52H's weapons capabilities is a replacement for the ageing AGM-86B Air-Launched Cruise Missile (ALCM). Originally slated for replacement by the AGM-129 Advanced Cruise Missile (ACM), the nuclear-armed ALCM is currently expected to serve until 2030, when it is planned to be replaced by the AGM-181 Long Range Stand Off Weapon (LRSO), which is intended to penetrate and survive

> **"The aircraft that equips today's Stratofortress Wings at Barksdale and Minot is a very different beast to the one that entered service in May 1961."**

B-52H Stratofortress 60-0050 assigned to the 419th Flight Test Squadron based at Edwards Air Force Base, California, on August 8, 2020. The aircraft is loaded with the AGM-183A Air-launched Rapid Response Weapon Instrumented Measurement Vehicle 2 prototype for a captive-carriage test flight over the Point Mugu Sea Range off the Southern California coast. US Air Force/Matt Williams

The AGM-183A Air-launched Rapid Response Weapon Instrumented Measurement Vehicle 2 prototype undergoes pre-flight procedures at Edwards Air Force Base, California, on August 8, 2020, prior to a captive-carriage test flight. US Air Force/Giancarlo Casem

integrated air defence systems and prosecute strategic targets.

Lockheed and Raytheon have been competing to design a new very-low-observable missile to replace the AGM-86 since 2017. Lockheed's contender was the YAGM-180A, while Raytheon's contender was allocated the designation YAGM-181A. Following design reviews, even before the technology maturation and risk reduction phase was over, in April 2020 the US Air Force announced plans to continue the LRSO's development with the Raytheon Company as a sole-source contractor. Raytheon was awarded a cost-plus-fixed-fee contract for the engineering and manufacturing development stage of the LRSO programme on July 1, 2021. The programme could see the procurement of more than 1,000 missiles,

which are projected to have a range more than 1,500 miles, with a total value of $2bn, though the FY2020 Defense Authorization Bill passed by Congress repealed the requirement for a conventional warhead version of the LRSO, leaving only the nuclear armed variant, meaning that production is likely to be much lower.

Instead of a conventional LRSO variant, the air force will use the AGM-158B JASSM-ER and the longer-ranged AGM-158D to fulfil the conventional standoff missile role. Development of the AGM-158D began in March 2016, when Lockheed Martin began analysis of an enhanced wing design to further increase the range of the AGM-158 missile. In September 2018, Lockheed was awarded a contract to develop an extreme range variant of the JASSM designated the AGM-158D, which is expected to enter service after deliveries begin in January 2024.

The new AGM-181A LRSO missile will use the W80 mod 4 nuclear warhead – developed as a life extension programme for the W80-1 and the warhead used for the AGM-86B and AGM-129 cruise missiles.

HYPERSONIC MISSILES

At the same time, the US Air Force is looking forward to being able to deploy an operational hypersonic missile, which promises to permit prompt global strikes from significant ranges while reducing the risks associated with forward basing. This is felt to be a key future capability, particularly in any possible future peer- or near-peer conflict.

Russia and China are among those working towards the deployment of a credible operational hypersonic air-to-surface

missile capability, while the US Air Force awarded a $985m contract to Raytheon Missiles and Defense for the development and demonstration of Hypersonic Attack Cruise Missile (HACM) prototypes in September 2022.

The HACM is a hypersonic air-launched weapon that will enable the US to hold fixed, high value, time-sensitive targets at risk in contested environments from standoff distances.

HACM offers a smaller form factor than the now terminated AGM-183 Air-launched Rapid Response Weapon for fighter integration and expanded bomber capacity, and thereby imposes cost on potential adversaries with additional complexity with vastly different trajectories than boost glide.

The HACM programme leverages investment made in the Southern Cross Integrated Flight Research Experiment (SCIFiRE), a bi-lateral US/Australian air-breathing hypersonic cruise missile prototyping effort which is a prelude to HACM.

The HACM programme will integrate advanced technologies and mature designs into an all-up round (AUR) prototype that will demonstrate a field-able long range prompt strike capability. It will also design, develop, manufacture, and test (in both the US and Australia) several prototype vehicles to inform future HACM acquisition decisions.

HACM will mature hypersonic technologies and processes to include subsystem integration, infrastructure and testing advancements, digital engineering, weapons open systems architecture, modelling and simulation, analytics, and high-performance computing environments.

In FY2024, the programme will utilize one company to build upon preliminary design activities and mature the HACM to critical design. The effort will continue with model-based engineering activities and the digital engineering ecosystem to complete critical design analysis, design verification testing, systems integration, lab development, initial qualification testing, initial flight test hardware orders, aircraft integration assets, and weapons open systems architecture compliance evaluation.

The US Air Force plans to deliver a HACM capability with operational utility by FY2027.

AVIONICS IMPROVEMENTS

But the improvements that will create the future B-52H are not only about the weapons that the aircraft will carry. Plans are afoot to replace the current APQ-166 radar with the APG-79(V)5 active electronically scanned array (AESA) radar under the so-called Radar Modernization Program (RMP), which completed its preliminary design review on-schedule on October 22, 2020.

The aircraft will receive a new, wide-band radome to allow full performance of the new radar, as well as two high-definition touch screen large area displays, two new hand controllers and two new display sensor system processors that will connect the radar with other B-52 systems. Initial operational capability on 11 B-52H aircraft is expected to be achieved in 2026.

POWER FOR THE BUFF

Flight-testing of a B-52H using a blend of synthetic fuel and JP-8 began in September 2006, as part of a US Air Force process to

Munitions maintenance technicians assigned to the 36th Munitions Squadron based at Andersen Air Force Base, Guam, conduct an inspection of AGM-158 Joint Air-to-Surface Standoff Missiles on, April 24, 2023. US Air Force/Airman 1st Class Spencer Perkins

B-52H 60-0050/ED assigned to the 412th Test Wing based at Edwards Air Force Base, California drops 2,000lb GBU-31 test articles from the underwing pylon over the Edwards weapons range. US Air Force

> **"The US Air Force has yet to specify a date when the B-52 fleet will achieve initial operational capability with the F130 engine."**

develop a more efficient fuel for its fleet, with less reliance on imported oil. The first B-52H flight using synthetic fuel (a blend of Fischer-Tropsch synthetic fuel derived from natural gas and JP-8) was made on September 19 at Edwards Air Force Base, California – with the new fuel powering two engines. The blended fuel was then used in all eight engines on December 15. The test aircraft (serial number 60-0034) arrived at Minot Air Force Base on January 17, 2007, for cold-weather testing, the last step in the certification process, and the B-52H was then certificated for the new synthetic fuel in August 2007.

Whatever fuel is used, the TF33-PW-103 engine that powers the B-52H has become increasingly difficult to sustain due to obsolescent technologies and diminished manufacturing sources. The US Air Force's Propulsion Directorate has projected that the engine will become unsustainable by 2030.

There have been several proposals to re-engine the BUFF over the years. There were different proposals for a B-52H powered by four engines, either the Rolls-Royce RB211 or Pratt & Whitney PW2000. In 1996, Rolls-Royce and Boeing proposed replacing the eight TF33s with four leased Rolls-Royce RB211-535 engines to reduce fuel costs, and greenhouse gas emissions, while increasing aircraft range and endurance. Unfortunately, however, using four big modern engines would have posed potential asymmetric issues, troublesome for the B-52's rudder to cope with, and the need for a complete rethink of engine controls and instrumentation.

When attention again turned to a re-engine programme, these difficulties were at the forefront of people's minds (both the RB211 and the PW2000 were no longer in production) and so the Commercial Engine Re-engine Program (CERP) called for the replacement of the eight TF33s with eight engines of similar size, weight, and thrust characteristics, with the aim of improving reliability and sustainment, and reducing fuel burn. Over an eight-year period, the programme was for 650 engines.

The CERP sought to use new commercial regional/business jet sized engines to replace the Pratt & Whitney TF33s and received proposals from GE Aviation of Evendale, Ohio, proposing variants of the CF34 and Passport engines, Pratt & Whitney of East Hartford, Connecticut with a militarised version of the PW800 (used by Gufstream business jets), and Rolls-Royce North America of Indianapolis, Indiana, offering a modified derivative of the BR725 – the F130, already in service with the US Air Force, powering both the C-37 and the E-11 BACN aircraft. In June 2018, the respondents were asked to provide evidence of their experience in providing this class of engines to customers, and their experience of tailoring the engines to individual customer needs.

New engines were to be digitally controlled, requiring new twin-engine nacelles, new pylons, and wiring to connect the powerplants to the B-52 cockpit.

It was hoped that the use of new technology and turbofan engines would increase the unrefuelled range of the B-52H sufficiently to allow the bomber to strike a target anywhere on earth from a base in the continental US (CONUS) with only a single aerial refuelling.

In September 2021 Rolls-Royce North America was selected to provide its F130 engine as the new powerplant for the B-52H under the CERP. Rolls-Royce will build and test the 650 F130 engines required at its Indianapolis, Indiana, facility.

Subsequently, in April 2022 – Spirit AeroSystems Holdings announced a contract award from Boeing to provide engine pylons and nacelles for the initial phase of the B-52 CERP.

By 2021 the CERP programme had increased in cost by 9% because of pandemic-related supply issues, and in May 2022, evidence to a House Armed Services Committee hearing revealed that the cost of the B-52 re-engine programme had increased by 50% because of integration issues. However, it subsequently emerged that this 50% cost differential was by comparison with a 2017 government estimate produced by the B-52 programme office (when the scope of the modifications was smaller), compared to the latest 2022 estimate.

US Air Force acquisition executive Andrew Hunter acknowledged that the cost increases were associated with the cost of integrating the engines on the B-52, which is a Boeing responsibility, and not the cost of the engines themselves. Rolls-Royce North America stated that there had been "no changes in engine pricing since the contract was awarded."

The risk reduction and prototyping phase will soon be completed, and that will allow the effort to become a formal acquisition programme. The US Air Force has yet to specify a date when the B-52 fleet will achieve initial operational capability with the F130 engine.

Defending

A B-52H parked on the flightline at Anderson Air Force Base, Guam, December 20, 2022, during a Bomber Task Force deployment. *US Air Force/TSgt James Cason*

Liberty

Mark Ayton provides an overview of the largest B-52H-equipped unit, the 2nd Bomb Wing based at Barksdale Air Force Base, Louisiana.

Shreveport is a city of some 400,000 people located in northwestern Louisiana. To the east of the city lies Barksdale Air Force Base, a sprawling facility that's home station to not only the 2nd and 307th Bomb Wing, but also Air Force Global Strike Command and the 8th Air Force. Barksdale is the largest bomber base in the world.

The primary unit on base is the active-duty 2nd BW (the 307th is an Air Force Reserve Command wing) with three flying units assigned: the 11th, 20th and 96th Bomb Squadrons. The 11th BS is the B-52H flying training unit, the 20th and 96th are operational squadrons, tasked with a variety of missions. Each operational squadron regularly locates to overseas bases for Bomber Task Force deployments and regularly conduct long-range missions of 20-hours or greater. The latter exercises the ability of the B-52 to hold virtually any target in the world at risk served by missions flown either from Barksdale or a forward operating location in European, Indo-Pacific or Southwest Asia theatres. This serves as a deterrent and gives the US President strike capabilities to meet the strategic requirements of many a crisis. Providing the deterrent is the most important part of the 2nd Bomb Wing's mission and their motto 'We Defend Liberty' underlines the role.

FLYING TRAINING UNIT

After completing their SUPT course with Air Education and Training Command, pilots selected to fly the B-52H arrive at the 11th BS for a 35-week formal training course.

In the classroom, students are taught procedures and then demonstrate them in simulators. After transitioning from the classroom to the aircraft itself, pilots perform multiple tasks including aerial refuelling, bomb runs, manoeuvring, defending the aircraft and landing.

It takes approximately 40 airmen to operate the squadron. While some of the instructors are assigned to the 11th BS, including civilians who are former active-duty B-52 aviators, many of the instructors are pulled from the 93rd BS, an Air Force Reserve Command unit based at Barksdale.

In September 2022, the B-52 Formal Training Unit (FTU), operated by the 11th and 93rd Bomb Squadrons graduated the first class of air crew using a new curriculum designed to operate the heavy bomber with a four-person crew instead of five. Currently, the B-52H has a navigator seat, a radar seat for the weapon systems officer, and an electronic warfare officer seat.

A weapons load team chief assigned to the 96th Aircraft Maintenance Unit latches a GBU-12 laser-guided bomb to the launcher within the bomb bay of a B-52H during Combat Hammer at Barksdale Air Force Base, Louisiana, June 7, 2022. Combat Hammer is an evaluation of the wing's capacity to generate, load and employ conventional weapons on target. US Air Force/Senior Airman Jonathan Ramos

Two members of a weapons load team from the 96th Aircraft Maintenance Unit load a CBU-105 munition to a B-52H during Combat Hammer. During the evaluation in June 2022 the 96th AMU loaded and employed five different types of munitions during eight sorties. US Air Force/Senior Airman Jonathan Ramos

Airmen assigned to the 96th Aircraft Maintenance Unit load an AGM-158 JASSM onto a B-52H during Combat Hammer at Barksdale Air Force Base, Louisiana, June 7, 2022. A key objective of Combat Hammer was to evaluate the reliability, maintainability, sustainability, accuracy, and readiness of complete fielded combat weapons systems against realistic threats and targets when employed by the operational air force. US Air Force/Senior Airman Jonathan Ramos

Students were instructed by different compartment instructors over several sorties to learn the various roles, so they are ready to sit in any of the offensive or defensive seats when called on. For now, both legacy electronic warfare officers and weapon system officers will have positions in the B-52.

The FTU is currently building the course such that new students graduating will be qualified to sit in all three seats of the jet until it is structurally modified for a four-person crew.

Graduates of the first course were the first cadre of B-52 instructors to hold all qualifications necessary and are trained to assimilate into the four-person construct that much easier.

DROPPING MUNITIONS

The 2nd BW squadrons continually practise flying into a particular target area to release weapons, which is a unique characteristic because manned bombers can be recalled up to the last minute before weapon launch, which allows the politicians to negotiate, think through or change the target set while the aircraft is en route.

B-52H aircrews must practise mission planning, scheduling, touch and goes, navigation, aerial refuelling, and bombing, and bring all skill sets together to successfully conduct long-range missions despite the fatigue, from Barksdale.

One drawback of staging long-duration missions is that squadrons cannot fly as many training sorties to and from Barksdale.

Given the B-52 fleet stands at 76 aircraft, additional strike capability can be provided by low-observable JASSM missiles or conventional air launched cruise missiles, a weapon unique to the B-52H, 5,000lb GBU-28 bunker buster munitions, and laser or GPS-guided munitions: the B-52H tends to use the AAQ-33 Sniper targeting pod to 'spike' targets.

B-52 aircrews must remain proficient in an ever-increasing mission set that includes close air support in permissive environments with use of the AAQ-33 Sniper pod and be able to hit targets accurately anywhere in the world, the key to long range strike.

However, a disadvantage of this very versatility is the required spin-up time which must be allocated between taskings to deploy to an ever-increasing number of places, otherwise the deterrent is lost.

But the most sensitive mission is nuclear strike the capacity for which must be maintained around the clock with no room for error, it's what's called a zero-defect mission category. Instructors and aircrew spend a long

> *"Providing the deterrent is the most important part of the 2nd Bomb Wing's mission and their motto 'We Defend Liberty' underlines the role."*

A B-52H assigned to the 2nd Bomb Wing at Barksdale Air Force Base, Louisiana undergoes maintenance at Andersen Air Force Base, Guam in support of a Bomber Task Force mission on April 9, 2023.
US Air Force/Airman 1st Class William Pugh

time training for the nuclear strike mission for which the 2nd BW commander must personally certify each one.

Despite its age, B-52 aircraft have not reached 50% of their service life and do not present lots of structural issues, in part because the aircraft were overbuilt. However, occasionally old wiring does create problems on the ground.

B-52 operators rate the aircraft as amazingly redundant, many of the systems are quad redundant. Similarly, those operators say there is no operational environment that the aircraft is unable to operate in employing the conventional air launched cruise missile (CALCM), a nuclear air-launched cruise missile (ALCM), or a conventional Joint Air-to-Surface Stand-Off missile (JASSM) with the capability to immediately target missiles.

The 340th Weapons Squadron based at Barksdale serves the B-52H force in just the same way as all the other weapons squadrons serve their respective communities, most importantly with integration. This includes some ground elements with all major stakeholders

Members of an 96th Aircraft Maintenance Unit load crew transport an AGM-158 JASSM to a B-52H at Barksdale Air Force Base, Louisiana. US Air Force/Senior Airman Jonathan Ramos

Aircrew prepare to board a B-52H Stratofortress at Barksdale Air Force Base. US Air Force/Airman 1st Class William Pugh

A B-52H assigned to the 2nd Bomb Wing takes-off at Andersen Air Force Base, Guam on April 9, 2023. US Air Force/Airman 1st Class William Pugh

> **"Manned bombers can be recalled up to the last minute before weapon launch, which allows the politicians to negotiate, think through or change the target set while the aircraft is en route."**

considering an effects-based attack, and not just striking the set target. What is the purpose of what the aircrews are doing? How do aircrew deal with the tactical, strategic, or operational problems? And when do they collectively conduct an effects-based solution to the challenge and understand how to use air power in the traditional sense - in a non-permissive environment, kicking down the door, so that the ground and naval components can operate in that environment.

BOMBER OPERATIONS
In February 2022, the 96th Expeditionary Bomb Squadron deployed four B-52H aircraft to Andersen Air Force Base, Guam for a Bomber Task Force deployment and undertook a variety of strategic missions including strengthening partnerships in the Indo-Pacific, engaging the joint force with close air support rehearsals, and refining tactics and techniques in a different geographic area of responsibility.

As a reminder, a Bomber Task Force enables different types of strategic bombers to operate forward in the Indo-Pacific region in support of the National Defense Strategy's objectives which are to enable strategic predictability and operational *un*predictability.

The 96th EBS began the BTF with participation in Exercise Cope North operating with the Japan Air Self-Defense Force, Royal Australian Air Force (RAAF), and the armed forces of the Republic of Korea.

During the BTF, the 96th EBS executed a range of joint operations with the US Air Force F-35A Lightning IIs and MC-130s in the South China Sea and coordinated multiple close air support munitions drops with joint terminal attack controllers in the region.

In August, 2022 four B-52H aircraft assigned to the 96th Bomb Squadron flew to Fairchild Air Force Base, Washington to undertake an Agile Combat Employment exercise held on August 16-19, and demonstrated a unique approach to delivering organic maintenance support.

Maintenance personnel assigned to the 2nd Aircraft Maintenance Squadron started their portion of ACE at Barksdale by packing the necessary repair, maintenance and replacement equipment into cargo containers known as the B-52 On-Board Cargo System, or BOCS and then flew on the B-52Hs to Fairchild.

A BOCS can hold up to 5,000lb of maintenance and support equipment, and connects to the bomb bays inside the aircraft. A B-52H can carry two BOCSs for an airlift capability of 10,000lb which can potentially reduce or eliminate the need for en route cargo support. Each bomber transported a five-person mobile maintenance team and a BOCS to practice the capability of landing, rearming, and repairing the aircraft anywhere that has enough runway.

A B-52H assigned to the 2nd Bomb Wing lands in the twilight at Andersen Air Force Base, Guam on April 22, 2023. US Air Force/Airman 1st Class William Pugh

On December 18, 2022, two B-52H aircraft from Barksdale Air Force Base, Louisiana, arrived at Andersen Air Force Base, Guam in support of a three-day BTF mission to highlight US Strategic Command's ability to strengthen extended deterrence capabilities throughout the Indo-Pacific region. The B-52H aircrews integrated with F-22s, KC-46 tankers from McConnell Air Force Base, Kansas, and a C-17 Globemaster III from Joint Base Charleston, South Carolina. It was the first integrated, long endurance flight as part of a BTF mission for the Air Mobility Command's new KC-46A Pegasus aircraft, which flew 42 total hours.

In March 2023, the 96th EBS deployed 190 airmen and four B-52H aircraft to Andersen Air Force Base, Guam for another BTF. During its month-long Micronesian deployment, the 96th EBS flew 412 hours and completed 29 missions, which included operations with the US Navy focused on enhancing maritime warfare.

A B-52H takes off at Andersen Air Force Base, Guam in support of a Bomber Task Force mission on April 14, 2023. *US Air Force/Airman 1st Class William Pugh*

A 2nd Bomb Wing B-52H parked on the flightline during Exercise Global Thunder at Minot Air Force Base, North Dakota, on April 11, 2023. Global Thunder exercises all US Strategic Command mission areas. *US Air Force/SSgt Michael Richmond*

"During its month-long Micronesian deployment, the 96th EBS flew 412 hours and completed 29 missions"

Minot's
Warbirds

Mark Ayton provides an overview of the B-52H-equipped 5th Bomb Wing based at Minot Air Force Base, North Dakota.

A B-52H Stratofortress assigned to the 23rd Expeditionary Bomb Squadron at RAF Fairford on August 28, 2020, during a Bomber Task Force deployment. US Air Force/Airman 1st Class Jesse Jenny

On March 14, 2023, a B-52H assigned to the 5th Bomb Wing (BW) flew over regions of the West African nation of Ghana. The bomber was participating in Flintlock, US Africa Command's largest annual special operations exercise. The exercise is staged to strengthen partner nations throughout Africa and to counter extremist organisations and provide security for their people. This year's event was co-hosted by Ghana and Cote d'Ivoire. The Minot Air Force-based bomber flew for more than 12 hours and 5,000 miles to reach Ghanaian skies:

a demonstration of America's global strike capability.

Last November the 5th BW participated in an exercise staged to test the wing's ability to stand alert and project combat power across the globe by conducting strategic-bomber readiness operations. Exercise Prairie Vigilance tested the 5th BW's security forces, maintainers, aircrews and command and control components as preparation for a response in the event of an attack against the United States and its allies.

In a similar vein, the 69th Bomb Squadron, one of two assigned to the 5th BW, undertook Exercise Knighthawk Thunder in which maintainers and aircrew responded to enemy action in simulated combat scenarios with

various weather conditions. Four B-52Hs took off twice during the exercise period to ensure aircrew and maintenance teams had opportunities to practice responding during a nuclear generation and achieve take-off as quickly as possible.

The previous month, two B-52Hs assigned to the 23rd Bomb Squadron transported 5th Aircraft Maintenance Squadron personnel, luggage, and equipment to Edwards Air Force Base, California for a Bomber Agile Combat Employment drill (BACE). The 5th AMXS airmen worked with US Navy munitions personnel who built and delivered Mk62 Quick Strike mines to the two bombers. The equipment flown to Edwards provided the 5th AMXS airmen with the means to receive the mines

> **"The Minot Air Force-based bomber flew for more than 12 hours and 5,000 miles to reach Ghanaian skies: a demonstration of America's global strike capability."**

and properly load them into the weapon bays. The personnel were able to load them onboard the two bombers using a minimal amount of equipment and manpower by comparison to other deployments and periods of temporary duty away from Minot.

BACE allows bomb squadrons to use dynamic force employment of personnel and equipment to practice and enhance self-sustainable operations for extended durations, and simultaneously maximise operational capabilities with minimum manning and equipment.

Minot Air Force Base in North Dakota is home station of the 5th Operations Group and two assigned B-52H flying squadrons: the 23rd and 69th Bomb Squadrons, each with an inventory of approximately 12 aircraft. The 23rd Bomb Squadron has the nick name 'Bomber Barons'.

The B-52H Stratofortress first entered US Air Force service over 60 years ago. After six decades of service, the type still supports the nuclear mission and undertakes a conventional mission set of close-air support, long-range strike, air interdiction, offensive counter-air, and maritime taskings, it's the primary platform for dropping naval mines.

FLYING A B-52

Squadron commander Lieutenant Colonel Michael Middents described the B-52 as an aeroplane that requires a heavy input from the pilot, and one that doesn't give an immediate response to those control inputs. He said: "Pilots learn to predict when to turn and the amount of input required to get to the desired location. On the screen, the flight management system displays a noodle in front of the jet to show where the aircraft will finish up on its current trajectory. For pilots who like to fly an aeroplane, rather than manage computer systems to fly an aircraft, the B-52 is a great aeroplane to fly. Besides flying the aircraft, the pilot is the maestro in an orchestra of crew dogs that are all trying to get different things done while trying to get to the target. Pilots flying this beast of an aeroplane must listen to the crew because they are trying to direct them where to go."

Commenting on what the B-52 is like to land, Lieutenant Sargeant, a pilot with the 23rd BS said: "It's not like anything else. It's a bit like landing a house sitting about 20 feet off the runway at touchdown. It's an interesting experience."

A unique aspect of the B-52 is its crosswind crab capability. Describing this trait, Lt Col Middents recalled when he was at Fairford when a three-ship got its taxi clearance: "The pilots synchronised their crosswind crab check, at which point the aircraft noses were turned to the left, but the gear is still straight ahead on the runway. When you are on approach to land, you find yourself facing the 11 or 10 o'clock position or the 1 or 2 o'clock position, yet you're guiding straight in line with the runway, and you take that aspect all the way to the ground. You're not looking at the runway as you're landing because it's over your shoulder."

B-52H MISSION SET

In addition to its extensive mission set, the B-52H can carry the widest array of weapons of any aircraft in the US Air Force. Explaining flight operations at Minot, Lt Col Middents said: "Day-to-day, we must train to that entire mission set. The squadron has a training team, a scheduling team and a weapons and tactics team. Together they ascertain the squadron's training requirements and plan for all aircrew to be ready when we are called up to do a tasking.

"Typically, we launch a couple sorties in the morning and a follow up in the afternoon. Once a month, we change our circadian rhythms and do a week of night flying during which our pilots conduct air refuelling, take-off, and landing training.

"Most training missions involve the use of a range and Joint Terminal Attack Controllers (JTACs), but when preparing to deploy we get a little bit creative and use either the Nevada (NTTR) or Utah Test and Training Range (UTTR). Each range has the capability to present a threat laydown to make the training more realistic. The NTTR is the only range that can accept some of the weapons employed by the B-52, such as cluster bombs."

For most training missions flown from Minot, B-52 aircrews use the Powder River Training Complex, the largest in America. Operated by Global Strike Command, its airspace extends over southeastern Montana, northeastern Wyoming, and western South Dakota.

During the squadron's most recent deployment work-up, B-52 aircrews worked with JTACs who were located on roads and highways for target talk-on procedures to structures and tracking their vehicles as they moved around, also to practice talk-on procedures.

A B-52H Stratofortress taxies on the runway on arrival at Minot Air Force Base from Al Udeid Air Base, Qatar, on September 10, 2021, at the end of a five-month deployment to the US Central Command theatre. US Air Force/Airman 1st Class Saomy Sabournin

Airmen transport an inert GBU-38 munition to a B-52H Stratofortress at Minot Air Force Base. *US Air Force/Senior Airman Armstrong*

"For pilots who like to fly an aeroplane, rather than manage computer systems to fly an aircraft, the B-52 is a great aeroplane to fly."

Training for a long-range strike mission launched from and recovering to Minot is more complicated. Flying from Al Udeid to Afghanistan is a three-and-a-half-hour trip into the Area of Responsibility (AOR). However, in a training scenario, it takes about 30 minutes to enter the range which means the crews need to be faster at getting their systems ready, weapons checked, and tactics plan read before execution.

Middents explained: "In a lot of ways, the training we do from Minot is a little more intense than what we experience in combat, which has its own challenges. We try to make it a little more intense for the aircrews

so, when they enter combat it's a step down for them. To exercise our full tactics, we need dedicated airspace so we can fully manoeuvre, and that's why we work with a range and choose targets within the range of our weapons to make it realistic."

MUNITIONS

Airmen assigned to the 5th Aircraft Munitions Squadron (AMS) based at Minot Air Force Base are responsible for storing, retrieving, assembling, delivering to the flight line, and loading weapons on a B-52.

Airmen with the 5th Aircraft Maintenance Squadron push open a B-52H bomb bay door to load weapons at Edwards Air Force Base, California. Due to the enormous weight, Airmen need to synchronise their efforts when opening the bomb bay doors. US Air Force/SrA Michael Richmond

BOMBER TASK FORCE IN ENGLAND

The last time the 23rd BS operated from RAF Fairford in England for a Bomber Task Force (BTF) deployment was in the summer of 2020.

The term Bomber Task Force refers to a deployment or employment of bomber forces in support of a theatre combatant commander's objectives. Bomber forces regularly conduct combined theatre security cooperation sorties with allies and partners to demonstrate America's capability to command, control and conduct bomber missions across the globe.

Discussing the concept of a BTF deployment, Lt Col Middents said in a perfect world, bomb squadrons would have a couple of months' notice beforehand deploying: "But there are plenty of occasions when we get a notice the same week, or just a couple of days before it's about to happen. In that case, we look at what's going on, talk with the planners at headquarters, and quickly put our plan together. So far, we've shown to be very adept at getting that done. We haven't had to cancel a single mission or deploy short of an aircraft. We are building BTF short notice into the culture and mindset of the crew dogs on the squadron. They know they need to be ready to go at any time.

"Last Christmas, we had nothing on the books. However, US Central Command had a need for bombers in the Persian Gulf region. Within a couple of days of notification, we were able to fly a 38-hour mission to the Persian Gulf and back again, but that's not a regular occurrence.

"After take-off, the first comment from a navigator on her first long mission was 'I guess this is home now'. It's an interesting crew culture life. You figure out what works for you to stay awake and what doesn't. Typically, we augment the crew with an extra pilot and an extra navigator so they can cycle their sleep to make sure they have the rest they need. You figure out what foods to eat and what foods not to eat. There's not a lot of room in the crew compartments but it's notable how creative the crews are in finding safe places to lay out and get some rest."

With eight thirsty Pratt & Whitney TF33 turbofan engines, a B-52 requires a lot of tanker

support for 38 hours in the air. Planners look at the mission and the route and use mission planning software to determine the amount of fuel required at different points. Options for the air refuelling plan differ. One option is to upload a lot of fuel in the early phase of the mission, another option is to conduct air refuelling throughout the mission. Diversion bases are essential if the crew is faced with a maintenance issue with any one of the eight engines or the four generators.

Lt Col Middents explained the tanker request process: "We pass our needs to the 608th Air Operations Center with 8th Air Force at Barksdale, who pass it to the Air Mobility Command's 618th AOC at Scott which issues details of our supporting tankers and their call signs. The 618th AOC is very good at pre-positioning tankers with the right amount of giveaway gas."

BTF missions can be tasked with just a few hours to go before the required take-off time. Getting each of the bombers tasked for the mission to an objective location and synchronised for a certain strike effect, takes a lot of coordination and planning before take-off."

For the transatlantic flight to Europe, the 23rd BS launched a six-ship formation from Minot, tracked toward and flew over Greenland, then on to the Norwegian Sea where Royal Norwegian Air Force F-16 fighters escorted the bombers. After integration drills, the six B-52s flew to the UK where they made an early morning arrival at RAF Fairford which took most people by surprise - a deliberate ploy by those involved.

"While at Fairford we flew missions to the Black Sea several times. On one mission, Russian Su-27s performed an unsafe, unprofessional manoeuvre in front of a B-52. The Su-27 pilots captured mobile phone video to try and show our B-52s were doing the wrong thing. The B-52 crew captured professional quality footage that clearly showed what the Russian Su-27 pilots did. On the same mission, an Su-27 from Kaliningrad followed the B-52s into Danish airspace, which was a significant international incident.

Of the nine different back shops in the 5th AMS, munitions control receives munition requirements for each mission, determines what is required and distributes the information to the shops. The conventional maintenance shop lists all the components required and then issues the information to the storage shop for picking. Some munitions and some components require testing. Those items are delivered to the conventional maintenance shop first so the team can inspect and test each item before the munition is assembled. Testing ensures the internal electronics and components are functioning correctly. Munition specialists follow technical orders for guidance through the assembly process. Assembly varies for each type of munition and typically starts with the munition's body placed on a stand. The crew start the assembly process by installing the internal plumbing, fuses, and run cables to the power supply. Components are hooked-up and torqued down, tail fins are fitted and tested to ensure the fuse and tail fins are connected and communicating with each other. Once functionality is complete, the assembly process is complete.

Inspectors work through a step-by-step checklist to make sure each munition will perform as intended. Finally, the munition is loaded onto a trailer ready to be towed by the line delivery section to a spot near the aircraft. The munition is in a safe mode with a safety pin fitted to each fuse and the dial set to that mode. Pins are removed and the dials are changed by ammo troops to the settings required for the mission. The munition is considered live but won't function until other prerequisites such as airspeed arming of the fuse have been met.

Master Sergeant Trapis Leslie, a section chief for conventional maintenance serving with the 5th AMS, said proficiency in assembling each of the many types and configurations of munitions is a challenge. Discussing some of the weapons, Leslie said the GBU-54 Laser JDAM which has a multitude of components, a laser designation capability, cables, and straps, is the most complex and time-consuming

Load crew members assigned to the 5th Aircraft Maintenance Squadron Weapons, load a Mk62 Quick Strike mine into the bomb bay of a B-52H during a Bomber Agile Combat Employment exercise on December 7, 2021, at Edwards Air Force Base, California. US Air Force/SrA Michael Richmond

munition to assemble, noting that 2,000lb class JDAMs are the largest conventional munition assembled by the maintenance shop.

Discussing the safety issues associated with munition assembly, MSgt Leslie said safety is the number one priority: "At the beginning of each assembly operation, we fill out a crew book with every hazard such as the munition's drop distance, a package or unpackaged distance that it can fall safely and go through the technical orders to check the warnings, cautions and notes.

"Each assembly is briefed by the crew chief to make sure everything is safe to handle. For example, when an inspector inspects the munition's fuses, they make sure the diodes switch to the disarmed position.

"As munitions are delivered to the maintenance shop, they are placed in the bay with the components. The crew use a table fitted with rollers upon which the individual components are fitted to the body in a sequence likened to a production line. Crew size varies from five to 30 people for a big mission.

"Munition specialists working for the maintenance shop use the integrated combat munition system to track each component. Using the computer-based system, maintenance shop airmen create a digital assembly of the components used once everything is physically assembled. Armament airmen who receive the munitions at the aircraft also have access to the system. They move the digital facsimile of the munition from the trailer to the aircraft, to complete a digital trail of the physical activities performed.

> **"In addition to its extensive mission set, the B-52H can carry the widest array of weapons of any aircraft in the US Air Force."**

A crew chief assigned to the 69th Aircraft Maintenance Unit conducts checks prior to a mission for Exercise Knighthawk Thunder at Minot Air Force Base, North Dakota, on January 12, 2022. US Air Force/A1C Saomy Sabournin

"There's not a lot of room in the crew compartments but it's notable how creative the crews are in finding safe places to lay out and get some rest."

Airmen assigned to the 705th Munitions Squadron load a B-52H with AGM-86B Air-Launch Cruise Missiles during Exercise Prairie Vigilance at Minot Air Force Base on September 16, 2022. The ALCMs were subsequently uploaded from the aircraft prior to take-off. US Air Force/Senior Airman Evan Lichtenhan

COMBAT OVER AFGHANISTAN

In early 2021, the 23rd BS was tasked to operate from Morón Air Base in southwest Spain for a BTF deployment. The squadron had undertaken the entire planning process to the point that its personnel were organising crew accommodation in the city of Seville. Picking up the story, Lt Col Middents said: "We were then told a situation was in effect in the CENTCOM area of responsibility. Eventually we handed off our plan to the 96th BS at Barksdale which conducted that mission. We were told there was a good chance we were going to the Middle East to meet the requirements of a request for forces, and we were required to be ready to deploy.

"At the time the execution order came from the Pentagon, we didn't have our order, and at the point when we started our engines, we didn't know if we were able to launch or not. When we thought it was time to shut down the engines, we got the order. Eighteen hours after the secretary of defense told us we were tasked with the mission, we had bombers at Al Udeid Air Base in Qatar. Upon arrival we hit the ground running, there had been no advanced party to figure everything out in support of personnel and flight operations. We figured it out."

The 23rd's primary mission was armed overwatch and to protect coalition and Afghan National Army forces with close air support, as US and coalition forces moved from locations around the country to Bagram Air Base near Kabul to airlift out of the theatre.

Detailing operations, Lt Col Middents said: "Four days after we had landed at Al Udeid, we generated our first combat sortie over Afghanistan. We had no weapons on the first sortie. It was flown for psychological effect to let the population know B-52s were back. Within a couple of days, we had armed aircraft over Kabul.

"We sent more crew members than were necessary simply to meet the close air support coverage time required. We started operations by flying three lines a day and maintained that ops tempo for several weeks. That took a toll on the jets, so we wound the ops tempo down a little. We then flew long, single-aircraft sorties to provide the same amount of coverage time, typically lasting 20-plus hours. Some crew members who flew the 38-hour mission said the 20-plus hours sorties to Afghanistan were more tedious and challenging. They were constantly engaged, flying orbits, using the targeting pod, scanning for targets, sometimes employing weapons, and going to a tanker for air refuelling every couple of hours.

"Squadron aircrews conducted 20 engagements when called in to help the Afghan National Army when its troops were under attack, though our mission was not to destroy or disrupt the Taliban. The overall mission was to support the withdrawal of the coalition from Afghanistan. Our crews often found a target, developed the target, but ultimately had to pass it to a different platform because the JTAC wanted a weapon that they could watch from shot to impact launched from an aircraft closer to the ground than our B-52s. That said, if there are multiple targets that need to be hit, a B-52 crew can develop all of them, load each into the weapons management system and strike all of them in a single pass.

"Usually, we would set-up in a circular or elliptical orbit overhead using the pod to try and find the targets. If we were able to drop from that position we did, otherwise we split from the orbit after developing the target on a direction that suited our weapon release. Then we turn back in from there. The last mission we flew over Kabul had several different aircraft in the CAS stack. Because of its capabilities, we were the first aircraft type on scene. We could observe anything that was going on from the periphery of the area and engage if required. We were also one of the last aircraft out of Afghanistan.

"Throughout the 2021 deployment to the CENTCOM theatre, whenever commanders and planners working in the Combined Air Operations Center at Al Udeid needed consistent close air support coverage, they called upon the B-52. When other strike options fell through, the commanders and planners extended the time spent on-station by the B-52. With two 12-hour VULs to cover, the B-52 was the most flexible option: it offered more firepower on a single jet over 12 hours." VUL refers to a vulnerability window which is the time an aircraft is on station, in this example to provide close air support.

Between April and September, 300 members of the 23rd Expeditionary Bomb Squadron supported and flew more than 3,100 hours and 240 combat sorties, the longest of which lasted for 22 hours. At the end of August, 2021 armed B-52s orbited overhead Kabul throughout the final days of US involvement in Afghanistan. It is notable that B-52s were some of the first US aircraft to operate over Afghanistan at the start of Operation Enduring Freedom, two decades earlier, in October 2001.

AGM-86B Air-Launch Cruise Missiles attached to a pylon on a hydraulic trailer used to lift and attach the pylon to the weapon station of B-52H 61-0005 during Exercise Prairie Vigilance at Minot Air Force Base, North Dakota. US Air Force/Senior Airman Zachary Wright

A B-52H assigned to the 69th Bomb Squadron taxies at Minot Air Force Base near to sunset during Exercise Knighthawk Thunder on January 12, 2022. US Air Force/A1C Saomy Sabournin

"Some crew members who flew the 38-hour mission said the 20-plus hours sorties to Afghanistan were more tedious and challenging."

The armament airmen must sign for the acceptance of the munitions to acknowledge receipt. The same processes used at Minot are used at a forward location where the facilities are often less extensive. For example, the crew might be working from an open pad with a munition assembly conveyor, a forklift, and trailers. Working with such a set-up, the assembly process may take longer despite the best efforts of the airmen involved."

MINE LAYING

At the time of our discussion, the 23rd BS was preparing to deploy from Minot to Edwards Air Force Base, California, where US Navy aviation ordnancemen were to build Mk62 Quickstrike mines and load them on B-52 aircraft for employment over the Pacific Missile Range off the coast of southern California.

Lt Col Middents said that laying mines is a very different mission because of the need to fly at very low level: "Proper airspeed control and timing is key for recovering the mines. We must be able to provide the US Navy with the exact splash points so Dolphins can be sent to tag each mine for its removal.

"Flying the B-52 at low-level is much more intense. Pilots find it quite exhilarating and fun. Each crew member has a specific role and every time you come up on a turn, every time you go through the turn, each member gives a timing call, a threat call, and call out any obstacles that might be in the way. The dialogue is running constantly. It gets a lot hotter in the aircraft and you start bumping around with the turbulence down low. You soon find out who can keep their lunch and who loses their lunch in a hurry. Physically and psychologically, it's a much more challenging environment to employ weapons. It's an eyeball and chart picking endeavour."

An airman tightens bolts on the pylon prior to lifting into position on a B-52H at Minot Air Force Base, North Dakota. US Air Force/Senior Airman Zachary Wright

Russia's Strategic Bomber Force

Alexander Mladenov examines the current state, operations, and inventory of Russia's long-range bomber fleet.

Russia's Air and Space Force's (RuASF's) Long-Range Aviation (Dal'naya Aviatsia - DA) arm is the most recognisable component of country's fearsome strategic nuclear deterrence triad. Furthermore, it is the only one endowed with a dual nuclear-conventional strike role, as its bombers could effectively be used in localised armed conflicts around the world at short notice.

DA's bomber crews train intensely in both nuclear and conventional precision missile strikes across a wide range of conflict scenarios and at any point on the globe, taking-off from their home bases in Russia or using forward operating locations in foreign countries. The strategic bomber community first showed its combat readiness and capability in the Russian campaign in Syria. It represented, in fact, the baptism of fire for the Tu-95MS and Tu-160 fleets, which had never been used in combat before.

DETERRENCE MISSION EXPLAINED

The DA is a powerful force at the disposal of Russian Armed Forces Supreme Commander, President Vladimir Putin, and is tasked to deliver effects in all strategic theatres where the Russian military could be involved.

In either a global or regional war it would be tasked to ruin the military-economic potential of the enemy state, striking its most important military and industrial facilities and infrastructure. The Tu-22M3 *Backfire-C*, Tu-95MS *Bear-H*, and Tu-160 *Blackjack* fleets would be called on to inflict irreparable damage through destruction of the enemy's important defence installations and disruption of government and military command-and-control channels and facilities.

The DA fleet is equipped with two types of strategic bomber, armed with long-range conventional and nuclear air-launched cruise missiles (ALCMs). The four-engine, swing-wing, supersonic Tu-160 *Blackjack* is primarily used for long-range missions where low- or high-level penetration of the enemy air defences may be required, while the four-engine turboprop, subsonic Tu-95MS *Bear-H* is deemed more suitable for missions where ALCMs are launched from standoff distances.

The third main type in DA service, and the most numerous, is the twin-engine, swing-wing, supersonic Tu-22M3 *Backfire-C*, which useful in low-intensity conflicts, it is a long-range heavy bomber which can be used for conventional or nuclear strikes, armed with long-range supersonic cruise missiles for knocking out sea and land targets in addition to free-fall bombs and sea mines. The Tu-22M3R *Backfire-C* long-range reconnaissance version is also in service with the DA.

The DA remains perhaps the best-funded arm within the RuASF, receiving all the funds needed to upgrade, overhaul and life-extend its aging fleet, re-launch production of the Tu-160 and introduce new-generation ALCMs. The DA also expects to get a new-generation

> *"The strategic bomber community first showed its combat readiness and capability in the Russian campaign in Syria."*

Plans to increase the Blackjack fleet are currently in progress, with ten newly built examples, in vastly enhanced configuration and known as the Tu-160M2, slated to be taken on strength by 2027, together with an upgrade programme, apparently set to cover 17 existing examples built between 1986 and 2018. United Aircraft Corporation

Russian political leaders and military commanders tend to refer to the highly visible and much-publicised global patrol operations by the Tu-160 and Tu-95MS force, combined with the mass introduction of new ALCMs, as Russia's non-symmetrical response to the US high-profile initiative to deploy anti-ballistic missile defence installations in Eastern Europe. Ministry of Defence of the Russian Federation

long-range bomber, developed under the PAK-DA programme, development of which began in 2013. PAK-DA is the acronym for Perspektivnyi Aviatsionnyi Kompleks Dal'ney Aviatsii or Prospective Long-Range Aviation Complex.

The maiden flight of this low-observable subsonic bomber is not expected to occur before 2025, followed by possible service entry in the early 2030s.

LONG-RANGE AVIATION ORGANISATION

In April 2009, the 37th Air Army of the Supreme Command (Strategic Purpose), controlling Russia's heavy bomber force, was reformed into the Long-Range Aviation Command (LRAC). In 2011, the LRAC also inherited the long-range strike assets of the Russian Naval Aviation (RNA) branch, represented by two Tu-22M3-equipped squadrons – one of these, stationed at Olenogorsk airfield on the Kola Peninsula in northwestern Russia, and the second at Kamenny Ruchey in the far east of the country.

The current DA structure, set up in December 2015, comprises the LRAC's HQ in

According to information exchanged under the START treaty, in 2017 Russia's nuclear-capable strategic bomber force comprised 25 Tu-95MS-6s, in addition to 30 more Tu-95MS-16s and 13 Tu-160s. Alexander Mladenov

"DA's bomber crews train intensely in both nuclear and conventional precision missile strikes across a wide range of conflict scenarios."

Moscow, two heavy bomber aviation divisions, one combat training and aircrew conversion centre and various auxiliary air units for liaison, training, transport and search and rescue (SAR).

Headquartered at Engels in southern Russia, the 22nd TBAD is a heavy bomber aviation division which controls three heavy bomber aviation regiments. Two of these are stationed at Engels and the third is at Shaykovka. In addition, the division controls another composite aviation regiment, the 40th SAP, stationed at Olenogorsk, which includes one Tu-22M3-equipped squadron and one transport and SAR squadron.

The 326th TBAD has its HQ at Ukrainka in Russia's far east, not far away from the city of Blagoveshtensk, and controls three heavy bomber regiments. Two of these are stationed at Ukrainka and the third is at Belaya near Irkutsk, in eastern Siberia.

The 43rd TSBPiPLS is a combat training and aircrew conversion centre, stationed at Ryazan-Dyagilevo south of Moscow. The same airfield is used to house the LRA's sole tanker regiment, the 203rd OGAP(SZ), while the 27th SAP is a composite air regiment equipped with transport, liaison and training aircraft and stationed at Tambov.

By December 2018, the DA fielded a strategic bomber fleet of some 17 Tu-160 *Blackjacks* in a single regiment with two component squadrons, in addition to about 60 Tu-95MS *Bear-H*s in three regiments, with a total of six squadrons. A few more examples serve with a squadron at Ryazan-Dyagilevo for conversion and upgrade training.

The DA also has two regiments, with six or seven squadrons, flying Tu-22M3 *Backfire-C*

long-range bombers. About 115 examples are on strength, including those held in long-term reserve, while the active fleet is believed to number no more than 45 aircraft, including those used for conversion and upgrade training at Ryazan-Dyagilevo. The *Backfire-C* fleet lacks an air refuelling capability and thus has no strategic significance. Its main purpose is to deliver heavy bomb loads during conventional conflicts and attack well-protected naval task groups in a blue water environment with conventional or nuclear supersonic missiles.

The current LRA Command organisational structure also includes an independent regiment (numberplate unknown), established in December 2021 at Soltsi airfield near Novgorod, it is equipped with MiG-31 strike aircraft armed with the Kinzhal air-to-surface hypersonic missiles.

In addition to the strategic and theatre bomber types, the DA also has a fleet of 18 Il-78 and Il-78M *Midas* air tankers. The auxiliary fleet comprises An-12 and An-26 turboprops, used for transport and SAR, Tu-134UBL and Tu-134UBSh training, transport and liaison jets, Mi-8 utility transport and SAR helicopters, Mi-26 heavy-lift transport helicopters and An-30B specialised photo survey aircraft.

LONG-RANGE POWER PROJECTION

The highly visible long-range patrol flights conducted in international airspace are deemed to be realistic operational training and at the same time a demonstration of global power projection. Such flights started on a regular basis in August 2007. Six years later, such bomber patrols conducted as a show of force were formally renamed 'flights conducted in accordance with the strategic deterrence plan of the Russian Armed Forces'. Between 2012 and 2017, the DA reported a total of 178 long-range/long-endurance patrol sorties.

The DA's most well-known international long-range patrol missions were flown to the Caribbean and Gulf of Mexico in December 2018, an undertaking which had previously begun in 2008. Such extended strategic bomber operations, including sporadic patrol missions flown from airfields in Venezuela,

In August 2018, a Tu-160 pair flew a patrol mission in the Arctic and Far Eastern regions for the first time, operating from a forward base near the Far Eastern city of Anadir, in co-ordination with Tu-142 long-range anti-submarine and maritime patrol aircraft of the Russian Naval Aviation. United Aircraft Corporation

NEW ALCMS FOR THE BOMBER FLEET

The DA has received two new types of ALCMs in the recent past – the Kh-555 and the Kh-101/Kh-102 - both developed by MKB Raduga for the Bear-H and Blackjack fleets. The conventionally armed Kh-555 is a vastly improved derivative of the 1980s-era nuclear Kh-55 (AS-15 Kent), the principal strategic bomber weapon used for the nuclear deterrence mission in the recent past. In turn, the Kh-101/Kh-102 is a new-generation stealthy ALCM family of missiles, much larger and heavier than the Kh-55 and Kh-555, providing longer range and better accuracy. It has been officially touted as an ultra-long-range strategic weapon, fielded in DA service in two versions.

The Kh-101 has a conventional warhead while the Kh-102 is fitted with a nuclear warhead. Powered by a retractable turbofan engine, the missile can fly up to 3,900nm and weighs around 5,300lb with an 880lb conventional warhead. Flying at cruise speeds up to 523kts at between 100 and 19,680ft altitude, the Kh-101 features terrain-contour matching (TERCOM) guidance, enhanced with INS/satellite en route correction (using a combined GLONASS/GPS receiver) and TV scene matching in the terminal phase of flight. This combined guidance method provides a claimed circular error probable (CEP) of between 30 to 60ft.

The Kh-101/Kh-102 was flight-tested for the first time in 2004 and commissioned into service with the LRA in 2013. The Tu-160 can carry up to 12 missiles internally on two rotary launcher units. The Tu-95MS, in turn, carries eight missiles on four twin-round pylons under the wings.

The smaller and lighter Kh-555, tested for the first time in 1999, has a range of up to 1,700nm and is fitted with a conventional warhead, weighing about 800lb, in both penetrating and cluster versions. Compared with the Kh-55, the conventional derivative features reduced radar-cross section and a much-improved guidance system, with TERCOM and INS/satellite en-route correction, plus a scale-matching area correlation system used in the terminal phase of flight. The claimed CEP for the Kh-555 is within 60ft.

A new medium-range ALCM type with a conventional warhead is currently in development at MKB Raduga, designated the Kh-50. It uses the same guidance system as the Kh-101 but has a smaller fuselage body with a further reduced radar cross-section. The missile is claimed to achieve a CEP within 15 to 21ft and can be carried in the weapons bays of Tu-22M3M, Tu-95MSM, Tu-160M and Tu-160M2 aircraft.

The Tu-95MSM will carry up to 14 missiles, including six in the weapons bay, while the Tu-160M and Tu-160M2 are each limited to 12 Kh-50s accommodated in the two weapons bays: the Tu-22M3M will carry between five and seven rounds.

Weighing 3,750lb, the Kh-50 uses a turbofan engine, has a cruise speed of 378kts and a maximum speed of 512kts. Its range is up to 2,600nm at altitudes between 150 to 15,000ft.

The conventional warhead comes in two versions – a penetrating version for striking protected targets and a cluster version, optimised for area target destruction. There is no information available regarding when the new missile will be commissioned into DA service.

During 2014, then commander-in-chief of the RuASF, Colonel General Viktor Bondarev, hinted that a new type of ALCM was in development – there is little doubt he was referring to the Kh-50, still a classified project. He described it as being capable of flying at ultra-low level and optimised for penetration of advanced air defences thanks to the artificial intelligence built-in to its advanced guidance system. Equipped with a highly sensitive radar homing and warning receiver, the Kh-50 missile will be able to detect and plot all radar threats along its pre-programmed route. Based on its smart guidance system, the missile will decide how to avoid these threats, following a route of best survival by turning left or right, at varying altitude and speed. To further enhance survivability when penetrating dense air defences, it is hinted that the Kh-50 can use a miniaturised radar jammer and towed decoys.

regarded as realistic training opportunities for the service's aircrews.

A certain proportion of the long-range patrol missions are reported to have been flown close to the eastern coast of the United States and Canada. According to the Ministry of Defence of the Russian Federation press releases, *Blackjack* and *Bear-H* crews have never behaved provocatively in any way during such flights. On one occasion in 2014, Russian *Bear-H* bombers continued further south down the US west coast to a point off the coast of California. In 2014, the DA branch also reported its first long-range patrols over the Mediterranean and South China Sea, reaching Guam, while in December 2017 the arm further expanded the geography of its patrol missions, operating from a temporary forward base in Indonesia.

UKRAINE

Combat operations in Ukraine showed, however, that it is necessary to launch multiple missiles against a single high-value target to gain penetration of the enemy ground-based air defences (GBAD) and deliver the desired kinetic effect when hitting the target. In Ukraine, the Kh-101 (AS-23A *Kodiak*), the main type of ALCM missile employed by the LRA bombers, proved to be effective thanks to its powerful warhead and reasonable accuracy, but its survivability was much less than originally expected due to the highly effective and innovative Ukrainian GBAD protecting high-value facilities in important urban and industrial centres. The Kh-101 proved especially useful for knocking out important infrastructure facilities such as thermal and hydropower stations and electrical sub-stations, receiving critical damage even in the case of a single missile hit.

In addition to the Kh-101, strike operations against Ukraine involved limited use of older Kh-55 and Kh-555 (AS-15A and AS-15B *Kent*) missiles, several of which were discovered at locations in Ukraine after falling to the ground. There were at least three known occasions when Kh-55 or Kh-555s were discovered on the ground in Ukraine lacking warheads

Nicaragua, and Cuba, became an integral component of the service's increasingly realistic combat training plan. According to the Russian defence minister, Sergey Shoigu, Russia needs to ensure military presence deep into the western Atlantic and eastern Pacific oceans, including the waters of the Caribbean basin and the Gulf of Mexico.

The benefit of these expensive global bomber patrol and training operations – conducted well beyond Russia's borders – is aircrew mission training. In 2017, DA flying units amassed 20,000 flight hours and each aircrew logged on average 120 flight hours, while the figures for 2018 called for the same total flight time, with aircrew average flight time reported to have exceeded 100 hours.

According to Lieutenant General Sergey Kobylash, DA Commander, the global patrols are conducted in international airspace, in full compliance with International Civil Aviation Organisation rules and procedures, without violating other countries' sovereignty. The intercepts and shadowing of the Russian bombers, undertaken by NATO Quick Reaction Alert fighters during patrols over neutral waters in the Atlantic and Pacific, are also

A total of 66 ALCM strikes were mounted by the LRA's Tu-160s and Tu-95MS' during the Syrian campaign, between November 2015 and September 2017. via Alexander Mladenov

A Tu-22M3 upgraded with the SVP-24-22 sub-system pictured dropping a 550lb (250kg) iron bomb. The add-on sub-system enables precise navigation bombing using dumb bombs and demonstrated good performance during the Syrian campaign. *Andrey Zinchuk*

> ## "As many as 30 aircraft were earmarked to be cycled through the Tu-22M3M upgrade under a new contract which was expected to be signed in 2020 or 2021."

but instead equipped with a mock-up of a nuclear warhead featuring the same shape and weight. Use of decoy missiles serve to be engaged by Ukraine's air defences, allowing follow-on missiles, fitted with a real warhead, to easily penetrate through the GBAD defensive zones and safely reach their intended targets.

The Tu-22M3 fleet was also used to strike Ukrainian targets, with the first operations reported on April 15. Tu-22M3s undertook carpet-bombing of the besieged Azovstal mega steel works in Mariupol, defended by

Ukraine's elite Azov brigade. *Backfire-C*s assigned to the 52nd TBAP, operating from their home base at Shaykovka, dropped FAB-500 free-fall bombs to destroy the massive industrial buildings and disrupt the defenders in the system of underground shelters and tunnels.

Another first for the *Backfire-C* fleet was use of the Kh-22 and Kh-32 ALCMs against surface targets. The first launches were made around May 11, 2022. In contrast to the Kh-101, Kh-555 and Kalibr-P, these heavy and bulky missiles, with cruise speeds

up to Mach 4.6 and a cruise altitude of 82,000ft, proved capable of survival against Ukraine's GBAD, with no shoot downs reported so far.

Kh-22 and Kh-32 missiles proved, however, to be notorious weapons, inflicting lots of collateral damage and civilian causalities, due to low accuracy and a destructive 2,000lb warhead. These radar-guided missiles were originally designed to strike ships: their repurposing to strike land targets resulted in poor accuracy with a circular error probable of almost 2,000ft.

A Tu-95MS named Dubna seen here resting at its home base in Engels, where the 184th TBAP is based. *via Alexander Mladenov*

The Tu-95MS fleet is set to receive new engines with more efficient propellers, as part of a major upgrade effort to boost range/endurance and take-off performance. Alexander Mladenov

measures to boost the availability rate of the DA fleet to 80% by 2017. There is no firm information as to whether the target was reached.

Currently, the fleet can be considered as being mature, with an average age of about 30 years. In 2009, the DA launched a series of small-scale upgrade initiatives to enable its *Bear-H* and *Blackjack* fleets to use new-generation ALCMs. In addition, a proportion of the *Backfire-C* fleet was upgraded to deploy another new-generation long-range missile and accurately deliver conventional free-fall bombs, with the installation of a new navigation/attack sub-system.

All three bomber types are set to undergo the upgrades in two phases. During the first phase they are receiving minor improvements to their navigation/attack sub-systems – mostly to replace obsolete avionics components and other out of production on-board equipment. Known as the interim Phase 1 upgrade, this package provides better long-term availability rates and improved navigation capability. Phase 2 involves comprehensive upgrades of the avionics of all three bomber types, including integration of all-new navigation/attack, communication, and electronic warfare suites. Phase 2 also involves comprehensive service life extension programmes and powerplant improvements for the *Bear-H* and *Blackjack* fleets and a new engine for the *Backfire-C*.

TU-22 BACKFIRE-C UPGRADES

Most of the Tu-22M3 aircraft remaining in LRA service were built in the second half of the 1980s, with the last *Backfire-Cs* rolling out of the KAZ Gorbunov plant in Kazan in 1993. The type is also slated for a significant upgrade to enable it to remain in service until the late 2030s.

The first small-scale upgrade of the *Backfire-C* fleet initiated in the late 2000s represented an unorthodox and affordable way to boost overall combat employment effectiveness in the bomber role using

GREATER ARCTIC PRESENCE

In addition to the long-range patrols conducted from their home bases at Engels and Ukrainka, *Bear-Hs* have used forward operating locations in Russia's extreme northern territories since the early 2010s. Vorkuta, Tiksi-3, Olenogorsk, Monchegorsk and Anadir in the far eastern territories are located beyond the Arctic circle.

In 2017, the Tu-22M3 force began flying regular patrols in the Arctic, using the forward operating bases at Anadir and Vorkuta. In turn, in August 2018, the Tu-160 force followed suite by launching patrols from Anadir airfield, some 430nm from Alaska. Using this forward operating location provides the bombers with extended mission endurance for patrolling over the deep-frozen Arctic and North Pole to simulate ALCM attacks against targets in North America. According to Lieutenant General Kobylash, the Arctic is considered to hold strategic importance for Russia and is the reason the DA has been tasked with developing new airfields and hardware, enabling the DA to effectively secure the country's sea borders in this important region.

FLEET UPGRADES

In June 2014 Russia's Defence Minister, Sergey Shoigu approved a package of

The Tu-22M3 Backfire-C can be used for anti-shipping missions, armed with the Kh-22 and Kh-32 long-range supersonic cruise missiles which can carry conventional or nuclear warheads and use active radar guidance. These are tailor made for employment against large warships. Ministry of Defence of the Russian Federation

conventional free-fall munitions. It received the SVP-24-22 modular digital upgrade package to provide accurate delivery of non-precision weapons. Developed by a Russian tech company named Gefest & T initially for the Su-24M *Fencer-E*, the upgrade package is built around a new digital mission computer, integrated with a combined GPS/GLONASS satellite navigation receiver, new hardware interface units and proprietary software for processing navigation data received from several different sources. The upgrade also features three new displays in the navigator/operator's crew station.

The SVP-24-22 provides precise positional information regardless of the mission duration which, in turn, allows accurate delivery of free-fall unguided bombs on targets with a known position. It is advertised by Gefest & T as providing accuracy comparable with that of laser- and TV-guided bombs. A Tu-22M3 prototype was upgraded with the SVP-24-22 in 2009 for test and evaluation, and four more *Backfire-C*s were subsequently slated for upgrade in 2012. By 2014, according to unconfirmed data, the number of Tu-22M3s upgraded with the SVP-24-22 had increased to seven, including the prototype. In 2014-2018, the system was also installed on some of the aircraft undergoing refurbishment and small-scale upgrade at both the KAZ Gorbunov plant and the 360 ARZ aircraft repair facility in Ryazan-Dyagilevo.

The small-scale upgrade of the entire *Backfire-C* fleet, within the frame of the Phase 1 upgrade effort, adding improved mission avionics suite and addressing obsolescence issues, was initiated in 2009 and the prototype was rolled out in 2012, with testing during 2013. The first production-upgraded *Backfire-C* was taken on strength in 2014.

Between 2014 and 2018, 20 to 25 Tu-22M3 aircraft were overhauled and cycled through the Phase 1 upgrade at KAZ Gorbunov. An undisclosed number of *Backfire-C* aircraft were also overhauled and upgraded to the Phase 1 standard at the 360th ARZ aircraft repair facility.

The Tu-22M3's upgraded mission avionics installed as part of the Phase 1 upgrade enables the aircraft to carry and launch new Kh-32 air-to-surface missiles. The Kh-32 missile has a range of up to 325nm and formally entered LRA service in late

This is the first Tu-95 upgraded to Tu-95MSM standard by TANTK Beriev in Taganrog. The first flight in the new guise reportedly occurred on August 22, 2020. TANTK Beriev

Blackjack and Bear-H crews received their baptism in fire during the Russian campaign in Syria, with the first combat sorties reported on November 17, 2015. They launched real-world combat Kh-555 ALCMs, together with the brand-new and longer-range Kh-101, for the first time. Alexander Mladenov

2016. Fitted with an active radar seeker, the Kh-32 missile was originally developed for use against maritime targets (replacing the obsolete Kh-22 or AS-4 *Kitchen*) but can also be employed against large radar-reflecting

land targets and comes equipped with conventional or nuclear warheads.

A contract for the Phase 2 upgrade was signed in 2016 and covers four *Backfire-C*s to the new standard. The first fully upgraded Tu-22M3M, incorporating Phase 2 standard mission avionics and electronic warfare suites, was rolled out at KAZ Gorbunov plant in August 2018. There is a high commonality between the Phase 2 mission equipment and that planned for integration on the Tu-160M2. The tail gun turret is removed, and unconfirmed reports state the upgraded *Backfire-C* will also receive an in-flight refuelling probe. There are also hints that the fully upgraded *Backfire-C* will be powered by the Tu-160M2's NK-32-02 engines, extending range to 5,400nm, but the first prototype at least did not include the new engines.

According to Tupolev, 80% of the aircraft's avionics suite is new, including the navigation, communication, electronic warfare and targeting suites as well as the engine and fuel management systems.

Service life of the upgraded aircraft is planned to be extended to 45 or even 50 years according to Tupolev's Konyukhov, while its weapons arsenal will most likely be enhanced with the new Kh-50 ALCM. It is

The Tu-22M's small-scale upgrade work under Phase 1, combined with airframe/general systems major inspections/overhauls and, in some cases, installation of the SVP-24-22 sub-system, were carried out in parallel at KAZ plant in Kazan and 360 ARZ plant in Ryazan. Andrey Zinchuk

also expected the bomber in its new guise will be capable of deploying both guided and unguided bombs.

However, the ambitious upgrade effort is still lagging the original schedule, with the roll-out of the Tu-22M3M prototype at KAZ Gorbunov plant occurring in August 2018, and the first flight reported on December 28, 2018.

A comprehensive testing effort should take about three years, while the production upgrade is slated to run in parallel with the flight-testing effort. This approach was expected to result in the first deliveries of fully upgraded *Backfire-C*s to front-line units around 2022.

As many as 30 aircraft were earmarked to be cycled through the Tu-22M3M upgrade under a new contract which was expected to be signed in 2020 or 2021.

TU-95 BEAR-H *UPGRADES*

The Tu-95MS fleet, rolled out between 1983 and 1991, has been little-used in terms of flight hours and is deemed to be in good technical condition in terms of airframe fatigue and corrosion damage but it is suffering from some powerplant and avionics obsolescence issues.

Currently, the *Bear-H* fleet is being cycled through a small-scale upgrade carried out at Tupolev's experimental plant in Zhukovsky near Moscow and TANTK Beriev in Taganrog. Known as the Phase 1 upgrade, it was launched in 2009 and includes new avionics to replace obsolete navigation and display systems, and new fuel system components. The upgraded aircraft have the capability to launch the new Kh-101/Kh-102 ultra-long-range cruise missiles, eight of which can be carried on four twin underwing launchers.

As many as 13 upgraded *Bear-H*s were delivered in 2015-2016, complemented by at least two more examples in 2017 and another four examples joined the fleet in 2018. Most, if not all the Tu-95MS aircraft in the active fleet are earmarked to cycle through the Phase 1 upgrade. During 2016, Lieutenant General Zhikharev revealed that 43 Tu-95MS aircraft will undergo an avionics upgrade, but this is

thought to refer to a comprehensive follow-on upgrade, known as Phase 2.

As Alexander Konyukhov, director general of Tupolev revealed in October 2018, work on Phase 2 of the *Bear-H*'s upgrade to the Tu-95MSM standard, is being carried out by the Taganrog-based TANTK Beriev company. The first flight was tentatively slated for late 2019, but the programme incurred delay and the first flight was reported in August 2020. The testing and evaluation stage was expected to last for two to three years while in August 2021 the Ministry of Defence of the Russian Federation announced the signature of the first production contract for the Tu-95MSM, involving an undisclosed

number of aircraft, but no delivery schedule had been revealed.

The Tu-95MSM upgrade contract, covering the full package of Phase 2 improvements, was signed by Tupolev and the Ministry of Defence of the Russian Federation in June 2018. The scope of the work calls for integration of an all-new navigation suite, including the Novella-NV1.021 search radar plus new optronic and electronic/signal intelligence systems. The upgraded *Bear-H* is also earmarked to introduce the new Meteor-NM2 self-protection suite featuring a new-generation radar jammer.

The Tu-95MSM will also introduce uprated NK-12MPM engines, fitted with AV-60T

PAK-DA FACING DELAYED DEVELOPMENT

The long-term future of Russia's strategic bomber force is dependent on the successful development of the PAK-DA, a new-generation four-engine, low-observable subsonic bomber. PAK-DA is a strategic deterrent system, currently being developed by Tupolev, a company controlled by Russia's United Aircraft Corp under a classified programme. Very few details have been revealed to date. Incorporating cutting-edge technologies, the PAK-DA is being designed with the primary objective of performing the entire range of missions currently assigned to the Tu-22M3, Tu-95MS and Tu-160 fleets.

According to Lieutenant General Anatoly Zhikharev, former commander of the DA, the PAK-DA aircraft is configured as a subsonic flying wing without fins. Its maximum take-off weight is 529,000lb, with a payload up to 66,000lb and a range of about 8,100nm without aerial refuelling.

The PAK DA is set to be powered by four non-afterburning engines, a derivative of the Tu-160's Kuznetsov NK-32 featuring new technologies to boost thrust and improve fuel efficiency. The new bomber is required to carry a greater payload than the Tu-160. The PAK-DA will feature all-new electronic warfare and communication suites,

and a new-generation navigation/attack suite. Its principal weapon will be the nuclear Kh-50 ALCM, which is currently under development.

The PAK-DA is expected to replace the existing fleet of 65 or so Tu-95MS Bear-H bombers which are in service with the RuASF.

The aircraft's development is being undertaken in accordance with a contract signed between the United Aircraft Company and the Ministry of Defence of the Russian Federation in December 2013. According to Lt Gen Zhikharev, it was originally slated to make its maiden flight in 2019. Followed in 2021, by joint state testing and evaluation undertaken by the RuASF Flight Testing Centre at Akhtubinsk. That same year, the PAK-DA was expected to enter production at KAPO plant in Kazan.

According to Yury Borisov, the former Russian vice prime minister responsible for supervising the country's military-industrial complex, PAK-DA's development and ground testing will be a protracted undertaking with a maiden flight expected in the 2025-2026 timeframe and the start of series production in 2028-2029.

This schedule, however, turned out to be over optimistic and the PAK-DA bomber is not expected to make its maiden flight before 2027.

The Engels-based Tu-95MS' and Tu-160s currently conduct a significant proportion of their long-range patrols over the deep-frozen Arctic, including the territories around the North Pole and the northern parts of the Atlantic Ocean, while occasionally venturing to the northern Pacific, reaching the Alaskan coast.
via Alexander Mladenov

"The Bear-H *fleet is set to continue in LRA service in both the nuclear deterrence and conventional long-range strike roles until the 2035-3040 timeframe."*

Since 2010, flight training of DA units has been notably intensified and all Tu-160 commander pilots log more than 100 flight hours a year, while the minimum figure set for the branch is 80 flight hours.
via Alexander Mladenov

The entire Tu-160 fleet, comprising 17 aircraft, is set for a major avionics upgrade, with the first example beginning testing in the new configuration in February 2020. *Alexander Mladenov.*

The major upgrade programmes conceived for both the Tu-160 and Tu-22M3 fleets foresee the use of common mission and flight/navigation avionics. *Alexander Mladenov*

The prop-driven Tu-96MS *Bear-H* is the mainstay of the DA's fleet, responsible for most routine long-range patrol operations. This upgraded to Phase 1 aircraft, named *Saratov* (a large city next to Engels), is from the 184th TBAP at Engels and sports external pylons for eight Kh-101 or Kh-102 ALCMs. *Alexander Mladenov*

propellers giving vastly improved take-off/landing performance and extended range/endurance. The new engine, rated at 15,000shp and driving the new and more efficient counter-rotating propellers, entered flight testing in April 2018. The effort was expected to be completed by the end of 2018 and deliveries of new engines for installation on upgraded *Bear-H*s began in 2020.

The Tu-95MSM upgrade package will also extending the aircraft's service life and see the introduction of new weapons, including the Kh-50 ALCM.

In its definitive upgraded form, the *Bear-H* fleet is set to continue in LRA service in both the nuclear deterrence and conventional long-range strike roles until the 2035-3040 timeframe.

TU-160 BLACKJACK UPGRADES

In December 2013, Lieutenant General Anatoly Zhikharev, the then DA commander, told the official newspaper of the Ministry of Defence of the Russian Federation, *Krasnaya Zvezda* (*Red Flag*), that the small Tu-160 fleet will continue in service for between 30 and 40 more years. This means the first of the original *Blackjack*s will reach retirement age somewhere between 2030 and 2040, while the late-production examples could be well-placed to serve even beyond 2050. The Tu-160s were built between 1986 and 2018; no fewer than nine examples were handed over after 1990, including one in 2008 while the last one arrived in early 2018. In fact, the latest news from the Russian MoD indicates the type's service life is planned to be incrementally extended by up to 50 years. The newly built and enhanced Tu-160M2s, the first of which was rolled out in 2019, are expected to continue in service beyond 2070.

According to Russia's Vice-Prime Minister Yury Borisov – who until May 2018 was the deputy defence minister responsible for the procurement - all 17 Tu-160s in the current RuASF inventory will be cycled through a comprehensive upgrade to Tu-160M standard during Phase 2, including integration of all-new navigation/attack and self-protection suites, and a glass cockpit.

A pair of Tu-160s flew a 25 hour-long and truly global patrol mission on September 19, 2020, which saw the bombers flying near Alaska and then returning to their home base at Engels.

The Syrian campaign saw the use in anger of all three DA bomber types, rushed in to combat during several surge periods between November 2015 and December 2017. *Alexander Mladenov*

As many as ten *Blackjack*s were slated to undergo the low-cost Phase 1, but the programme is experiencing delay. The prototype aircraft, named *Valentin Bliznyk*, was upgraded in 2006. The first Tu-160 with the production-standard Phase 1 upgrade package and named *Andrey Tupolev*, was handed over to the RuASF in December 2014 after completion at Tupolev's KAZ Gorbunov plant in Kazan. Two more *Blackjack*s were then upgraded to Phase 1 standard – named *Vasiliy Reshetnikov* and *Vasiliy Sen'ko* – and re-delivered to the LRA in January 2016 and August 2017 respectively. In 2018, another upgraded *Blackjack*, *Pyotr Deinekin*, was taken on strength, this a newly built machine, and in January 2019 *Ivan Yarygin* entered flight testing following overhaul and the Phase 1 upgrade.

Another improvement for the Tu-160 fleet is the new uprated NK-32-02 afterburning turbofan engine. Flight testing of a *Blackjack* powered by the new engines was originally planned for completion in late 2018 but the first flight powered by NK-32-02 engines was reported in November 2020.

Compared with the original NK-32, which dates to the 1980s, the new variant consumes less fuel, extending the Tu-160's range by around 540nm. The first pair of new NK-32-02 engines, produced at PAO Kuznetsov plant in Samara, was reported ready for shipping to the Russian MoD in early June 2018. The first contract calls for delivery of 22 new engines, most likely for installation in new-build *Blackjack*s.

The first new production *Blackjack*, named *Pyotr Deinekin*, used an incomplete airframe originally built in the 1990s and featured the Phase 1 avionics suite. The aircraft took to the air for the first time from the factory airfield

The Backfire-C has limited flight endurance and range compared to the Blackjack and Bear-H due to the lack of air refuelling capability, but this is still sufficient for effective power projection in the Baltic and Black Seas and the Northern Atlantic. Ministry of Defence of the Russian Federation

of Tupolev's KAZ Gorbunov plant on January 25, 2018. It is slated for a follow-on upgrade to the enhanced Tu-160M2 standard, covering all Phase 2 improvements, including a glass cockpit.

The first Tu-160, overhauled and upgraded to the Tu-160M standard (also referred to as Tu-160M1 by some sources in Russia), was expected to be rolled out in the third quarter of 2019, with the first flight reported in February 2020 while in November that year it began flying with the new NK-32-02 engines. The flight testing and evaluation of the upgrade package is expected to run for at least three years. The second Tu-160 to receive the Phase 1 upgrade began flight testing in September 2021 and the third example followed in December 2022, while the fourth was set to begin flight testing in early 2023.

The first production-standard upgraded Blackjacks were not expected to be taken on strength by the VKS before 2023.

The definitive new-generation Blackjack for the DA, dubbed Tu-160M2, features the Phase 2 avionics package and will be new-build aircraft. The first was tentatively scheduled to

RUSSIAN LONG-RANGE AVIATION COMMAND ORDER OF BATTLE		
Unit	Base	Types
Headquarters	Moscow	
Centrally-reporting units		
43rd TsBPiPLS	Ryazan-Dyagilevo	An-26, Tu-22M3, Tu-95MS
203rd OGAP(SZ) with two component tanker squadrons	Ryazan-Dyagilevo	Il-78, Il-78M
27th SAP with two or three component transport squadrons	Tambov	An-12, An-26, An-30, Tu-134 UBL, Tu-134Sh, Mi-8T/MT
22nd Guards Heavy Bomber Aviation Division	Engels	
121st TBAP with two component bomber squadrons	Engels	Tu-160
184th TBAP with two component bomber squadrons	Engels	Tu-95MS
52nd TBAP with two component bomber squadrons	Shaikovka	Tu-22M3, Tu-22M3R
40th SAP with one bomber and one transport/SAR squadron	Olenogorsk	Tu-22M3, An-12, Mi-8, Mi-26
326th Heavy Bomber Aviation Division	Ukrainka	
182nd TBAP with two component bomber squadrons	Ukrainka	Tu-95MS
79th TBAP with two component bomber squadrons	Ukrainka	Tu-95MS
200th Guards TBAP with three component bomber squadrons and one transport squadron	Belaya	Tu-22M3, Tu-22M3R, An-12, An-26, An-30

Note: Compiled using publicly available sources only and covering the DA main units. No official information has been released on the LRAC order of battle since the latest round of changes undertaken in 2015.

ABBREVIATIONS

BAP	Bomber Aviation Regiment
OGAP(SZ)	Independent Guards Aviation Regiment
SAP	Composite Aviation Regiment
TBAD	Heavy Bomber Aviation Division
TBAP	Heavy Bomber Aviation Regiment
TsBPiPLS	Combat and Conversion Training Centre for LRA personnel

The Tu-22M3 force from Shaikovka southwest of Moscow has been deployed for patrol and power projection operations over the Baltic and Black Seas and occasionally conducts patrol missions into the northern Atlantic. *Ministry of Defence of the Russian Federation*

fly in 2019 but was postponed until the end of 2020. According to Borisov, serial production of the Tu-160M2, powered by the new NK-32-02 engines, should have begun in 2021 with a rate of three to four aircraft a year, with the first deliveries to the RuASF planned for 2023. The overall combat capability of the Tu-160M2 is reportedly twice that of the original *Blackjack* equipped with 1980s era mission suite and weapons. The Tu-160M2 will also feature a reduced a radar cross-section, thanks to new radar-absorbent coatings applied to the airframe.

As many as 50 *Blackjack*s are planned for eventual production but the first firm contract, signed in January 2018 between the Ministry of Defence of the Russian Federation and UAC (the parent company of Tupolev), covers only ten examples at a unit price of RUB 15bn (approx. US$185m): the contract guarantees work at KAZ Gorbunov plant until the end of 2027.

> "Incorporating cutting-edge technologies, the PAK-DA is being designed with the primary objective of performing the entire range of missions currently assigned to the Tu-22M3, Tu-95MS and Tu-160 fleets."

A Bear-H from the 184th TBAP at Engels, situated on the Volga, some 700km southeast of Moscow, is seen here during a training flight in the vicinity of its base. *Ministry of Defence of the Russian Federation*

XI'AN H-6

Alexander Mladenov and Krasimir Grozev provide an overview of the Chinese Xi'an H-6 bomber.

When the Soviet Tupolev Tu-16 bomber made its maiden flight in April 1952, it is unlikely that anyone believed the type would still be in series production nearly 70 years later, albeit in a deeply modified form.

Dubbed the H-6, China began assembling this twin-engine jet bomber under license in 1958. Throughout the subsequent decades the Chinese aerospace industry has built a dozen derivatives all like the original Soviet-era Tu-16 design.

In January 2007, a prototype of a deeply modified version was launched by the Xi'an Aircraft Industrial Corporation, which became known as the H-6K.

This is a radically re-worked derivative equipped with new Russian-made D-30KP-2 turbofan engines which, although not state of the art equipment, proved much more fuel-efficient than the original WP-8 turbojets. D-30KP-2 engines have been in service with the PLAAF for years powering its fleet of Il-76 airlifters.

As is the case with most turbofan engine upgrades, the D-30KP-2 significantly increased the combat radius of the Chinese strategic bomber to between 1,620 and 1,900nm. Modifications were required including larger intakes, a new nose, and a multifunction radar.

Two critical sensor systems are fitted to the fuselage underside: an electro-optical surveillance system and a more powerful electronic warfare system with antennas installed at various locations on the fuselage. Composite materials are

used to lighten the weight of the aircraft's structure.

But the upgrade also enabled the crew complement to reduce from six to three: a commander, co-pilot, and navigator/weapons system operator, all accommodated on ejection seats. The tail gunner turret was removed, and an auxiliary power unit installed in its place.

In 2020, some H-6Ks were first seen fitted with two additional underwing pylons, most likely to carry pods housing electronic warfare systems. Prior, H-6s were configured with six underwing hardpoints used for weapons carriage.

The main H-6K weapon is the nuclear or conventionally armed KD-20 cruise missile with a range of 810nm, with a six-missile payload possible. Alternatively, four of the older 100nm-range KD-63 cruise missiles can be carried but doing so requires a datalink pod

"The main H-6K weapon is the nuclear or conventionally armed KD-20 cruise missile with a range of 810nm, with a six-missile payload possible."

A pair of H-6N bombers armed with KD-20 and KD-63 air-launched cruise missiles. The H-6N is the latest derivative of the bomber to enter production and is distinguished by the in-flight refuelling probe installed atop of the nose. *Chinese internet*

Chinese internet

> **"It would seem logical that the H-6N can employ the same arsenal of weapons as its predecessor."**

to be loaded on a small pylon underneath the rear fuselage.

Photographs of an H-6K armed with four YJ-12 anti-ship missiles first appeared on Chinese websites in 2020.

In addition to its ability to employ doomsday type missiles, the H-6K can also deliver conventional ordnance by releasing free-fall bombs from its bomb bay.

Following service entry in 2011, today five PLAAF bomber regiments operate the H-6K. Since 2016, those regiments have launched regular long-range missions over the South Pacific, presumably practicing missile strikes against American and allied air bases and ship formations.

At the end of 2016, a new derivative, dubbed the H-6N, began flight testing. Compared to the H-6K, the N-model has some notable differences including a nose-mounted in-flight refuelling probe (the first H-6 model with such a probe) and hardpoints installed on the centreline of its modified fuselage under side, probably for the carriage of a single air-launched ballistic missile of an unknown type.

Poor quality images posted on Chinese websites show that the H-6N is being tested with such a heavy missile. It is not yet clear whether the missile is intended to destroy stationary targets or can also be employed against ship formations. Chinese media outlets suggest

> **"Compared to the H-6K, the N-model has some notable differences including a nose-mounted in-flight refuelling probe."**

that the ballistic missile may be equipped with a manoeuvrable hypersonic glide vehicle.

It would seem logical that the H-6N can employ the same arsenal of weapons as its predecessor.

A military parade in Beijing on October 1, 2019, was the venue for the first public appearance of the H-6N. One fully equipped regiment is currently thought to be operating the H-6N.

H-6K 11097 undergoing maintenance at sunset. Chinese internet